ENDORSEMENTS

D0746025

PAUL ANDERSON, professor of biblical and Quaker
studies, director of the George Fox University
Congregational Discernment Project
Newberg, Oregon

There are lots of books out there telling you what *they* think God's
will might be; this one points the way to discerning the divine will
for ourselves. In theory and in practice, this book will be an
immense help to all leaders desiring to connect people with the will
of Christ for today. Case studies allow the reader to make parallel
applications for today, and scriptural teaching grounds the process
in biblical counsel and wisdom. What Fendall, Wood, and Bishop
have done is a great service to the church, but also to the world
beyond. They provide practical ways forward in the central issue at
stake in Christian leadership: how to lead in such a way that helps
people come to unity around a common sense of Christ's leading.
When that happens, it is not only a good day for the church; it is
more importantly a great new day for the world!

BEN STALEY, pastor
Northridge Friends Church
Wichita, Kansas

Practicing Discernment Together will be a helpful resource for all who
take seriously the awesome challenge of finding God's way in
decision making. Here is practical guidance for new church leaders,
experienced leaders in difficult situations, and the faithful pastor
who is expected to know how to resolve any given situation.

The authors should be commended for their insights and their
practical approach for navigating the decision-making process in a
culture highly influenced by individualism and relativism. I intend
to have our church leaders begin the new year by reading this
excellent book, which gives important guidance to individuals and
groups as they turn to God, remain attentive to his voice, and
courageously carry out his plan.

Are you looking for an alternative to political, polarizing decision making? This book is a vital guide to strengthen discernment within the covenant community.

Practicing Discernment Together has the potential to be a very useful guide to those seeking to change the way decisions are made within the corporate church. The authors do a great job of placing before the reader the essential attitudes and practices of a way of being that can enable groups of all types to be more attuned to the voice of the Holy Spirit moving among their diverse members, while aligning their choices with that discernment. Churches outside the Friends culture, not rooted in the tradition of discernment, face enormous challenges of language, culture, and tradition in initiating and sustaining the change the authors point toward. This book speaks to them in a way that many should be able to receive and act upon. As one who comes from a mainline Protestant denomination deeply grounded in the business/parliamentary model that seems to relish conflict worked out in intellectual debate, I especially appreciate the materials on the role of the clerk before, during, and after discernment. This is a book that should be a part of the library of every serious advocate of discernment. It is a very valuable resource for anyone seeking to lead his or her group toward a deeper commitment to understanding and doing God's will.

Founded on the principle of seeking and finding God's direction together, this book is an eminently practical guide for leading and participating in decision-making meetings. Complementing their well-considered outline of principles are indispensable bits of practitioner's wisdom that plead for a highlighting pen. The real-life case studies demonstrate that finding God's direction is attainable by ordinary believers even in especially difficult circumstances. Even better, congregations are transformed in the process of practicing discernment.

While it will be useful in a broader context, I expect this exceptional work will become a standard reference in Friends churches. Happily, required reading can be a delight, and is in this case. I pray *Practicing Discernment Together* will contribute to a revival of this Spirit-led practice in Christ's church, and subsequent transformation of congregations.

PATRICIA THOMAS, clerk of the Earlham School
of Religion (Richmond, Indiana) Board of Advisors
Wilmington, Ohio

Beginning with the bold premise that God gives us the capacity to know God's heart and will, *Practicing Discernment Together* leads the reader through the role of clerking a meeting and ways to participate as an individual in group discernment.

The joy and strength of this little volume is that it is full of sound theological truths, insights, and practical suggestions that caused this reader to grab not only my highlighter pen but also to fill the margins with asterisks and notes! The authors have struck a wonderful balance between solid scriptural knowledge, practical suggestions, and case studies to create an extremely useful "how-to" book. The reader comes away saying, "Wow! Now I see how group discernment is done. We can practice this in our business meetings!"

FREDERICK W. SCHMIDT, director of
spiritual formation and Anglican studies at
Perkins School of Theology and
author of *What God Wants for Your Life*
Dallas, Texas

In a world where an increasing number of people protest that they are spiritual, but not religious, Lon Fendall, Jan Wood, and Bruce Bishop give the church the tools to reintroduce spiritual principles into the task of discernment.

VICTORIA CURTISS, Presbyterian pastor
and church consultant
Portland, Oregon

This is the book I have been looking for to teach others about discernment and to hone my own skills as a facilitator. It offers excellent guidance using a framework and language that is easily accessible for a variety of church and organizational settings. Integrating wisdom from several faith traditions, the authors address the challenges of conflict, uncertainty, listening, waiting, and trust. From case studies to checklists, its tools build confidence to venture into the wondrous arena of being led by God's Spirit together. An inspiring gift to the church!

JOHN PUNSHON, author and lecturer
Milton Keynes, England

Full of wisdom, imagination, and sound advice, this little book is addressed to groups of Christians (and others) faithfully seeking God's guidance as a body. In part a meditation on Scripture, it is also a powerful explanation of how the Quaker decision-making process is actually an exercise in personal and corporate discernment. It will be valuable far beyond the limits of the Friends Church.

DAVID BRANDT, president
George Fox University
Newberg, Oregon

This volume is clear and very practical. It will be a helpful guide for churches wishing to make decisions by discernment for the first time as well as churches who have made decisions by discernment for many years. The inclusion of case studies inserts a real-world feel into a process that too often seems entirely theoretical to groups not used to making decisions through discernment.

The book's emphasis on the necessity of spiritual preparation is refreshing. Any decision-making process would be enhanced by such preparation.

Practicing Discernment Together is an important addition to decision-making literature for Christians.

JOHN BRAUN, pastor and leader
in Church of the Brethren, Mennonite,
Friends, and ecumenical settings
Seattle, Washington

Practicing Discernment Together puts the cookies on the bottom shelf for those of us who want our decision making to be empowered, unifying, and spiritually deepening. The authors have placed spotlights on all the pertinent steps for finding God's way forward, such that each participant feels validated and included. They have thrust the perceptual doorway wide open. From their rich backgrounds in guiding conflicted groups, they introduce underlying scriptural truths as dependable good friends. The book's case studies offer faith-renewing insights into God's trustworthy guidance through specific and complicated situations. It offers a hopeful ladder out of the pit of church politics that leaves Christians divided, discounted, wounded, and resentful. *Practicing Discernment Together* reunites us—individuals, group members, and leaders—with the heart of our God who is eager to turn every looming problem into an opportunity for growth and discovery. I am eager to place this book into many hands.

JEFF DAVIS, director of corporate stewardship,
Evangelical Friends Church Southwest
Yorba Linda, California

I recommend this immensely practical book to help Christian leaders cultivate godly discernment within the context of a group, small or large. *Practicing Discernment Together* is filled with useful instruction to empower any group to effectively listen to God's voice and discern his particular will.

AUTHORS

The authors are available for consulting service and public presentations.

LON FENDALL
director of the Center for Global Studies
and the Center for Peace and Justice,
George Fox University
lfendall@georgefox.edu

My "day job" is teaching at George Fox University in Newberg, Oregon, and directing the university's Center for Peace and Justice and the Center for Global Studies. While this work is rewarding, I also find joy in my work with Good News Associates (GNA), a ministry founded and directed by coauthor Jan Wood. Being a part of GNA gives me a supportive community for my writing and opens doors for teaching and speaking. Jan, Bruce, and I have presented workshops on discernment and decision making a number of times, and we are pleased to see the multiplication of this effort through *Practicing Discernment Together*. I am happy to respond to speaking-engagement requests and inquiries about the content of this book and the other books I have authored or coauthored—*Unlocking Horns*, *At Home with the Poor*, *Citizenship*, and *To Live Free*.

JAN WOOD
executive director,
Good News Associates
janwood@goodnewsassoc.org

I find that making decisions together through discernment is an effective way to discover God's leadings and a life-giving and practical way to do the business of any organization. I was raised in Friends churches, so I was fortunate to receive the tools for discernment early in my life. As a pastor, college administrator, and in my present position as executive director of Good News Associates, I have had wonderful opportunities to help groups work together. It is my joy to come alongside churches, denominations, businesses, and nonprofit organizations as a consultant to teach and coach group discernment process. I delight in helping organizations live joyfully and effectively into the fullness of their missions. I am also the author of *Christians at Work—Not Business as Usual*.

BRUCE BISHOP
interim associate superintendent,
Northwest Yearly Meeting of Friends
bbishop@nwfriends.org

Currently I am the interim associate superintendent of Northwest Yearly Meeting of Friends (NWYM). Encouraged by the understanding of Friends and my own experience growing up in the Friends community, I've made spiritual discernment a priority. For the last several years I've been helping Friends relearn the theology and practice of discernment, offering workshops and practicums around personal and corporate spiritual discernment. As clerk of the elders at my local church, I've had the opportunity to practice what I preach, moving it from a task-oriented committee to a discernment-based community. I desire to become increasingly sensitive to the stirrings of God in my life and to help others do so as well. It has been a great joy to help people uncover and verbalize their experiences of God's voice.

Practicing Discernment Together

*Finding God's Way Forward
in Decision Making*

by
Lon Fendall
Jan Wood
Bruce Bishop

BARCLAY PRESS
Newberg, Oregon

PRACTICING DISCERNMENT TOGETHER
Finding God's Way Forward in Decision Making

© 2007 by Lon Fendall, Jan Wood, and Bruce Bishop

Published by Barclay Press
211 N. Meridian St., #101, Newberg, OR 97132
www.barclaypress.com

ISBN 1-59498-009-8

All Scripture quotations, unless otherwise indicated, are taken from the
Holy Bible, New International Version®. NIV®. Copyright © 1973, 1978, 1984 by
International Bible Society. Used by permission of Zondervan.
All rights reserved.

Scripture verses marked KJV are from the King James Version of the Bible.
Those marked ESV are from *The Holy Bible, English Standard Version.*
Copyright © 2000, 2001 by Crossway Bibles, a division of Good News Publishers.
Used by permission. Scripture quotations marked CEV are from the *Contemporary
English Version* © 1991, 1992, 1995 by American Bible Society. Used by permission.
Those marked *The Message,* copyright © by Eugene H. Peterson 1993, 1994, 1995,
1996, 2000, 2001, 2002, are used by permission of NavPress Publishing Group.

Cover design by Dan Jamison

CONTENTS

PREFACE

Words are like 18-wheelers; they come in all shapes and sizes and are meant to haul freight. Words convey that freight via books, ideas, concepts, convictions, and passions. This particular book looks at and "unpacks" the concept of discernment—that imperfect and sometimes wonderful process of finding clarity about God's leading.

We have used the phrase "way forward" in the subtitle of the book after observing the journeys of many Christian organizations. Endless road hazards, detours, confusing signs, and unforeseen dangers lie in wait on these journeys of decision making. We wrote this book as a map to provide guidance to groups so that they reach their destinations with joy.

While we were growing up, service stations had state and city maps available for travelers. Today we can easily find maps on Web sites that not only give accurate information about each intersection and road name, but that warn about road hazards and invite us to partake of amenities along the way. We hope this book is that kind of practical, interactive, and reliable map for Christian decision making.

We look primarily at the discernment that happens when groups of Christ's followers get serious about being God's people. They feel so passionate about this pursuit that they cannot be content with practicing discernment only in their individual spiritual growth and obedience. They understand that God the Holy Spirit speaks not only to individuals, but also to groups of believers.

This book owes its existence to the authors' joyful and frustrating experiences with group decision making. The joyful experiences have filled us with the wonder of seeing God at work—bringing people of many different backgrounds, ideologies, personalities, and biases into a place of agreement on God's way forward. The frustrating experiences have come in the same settings, but with much less satisfactory results. The same kinds of differing backgrounds, ideologies, personalities, and biases made their way into the "mixing bowl" of decision making in Christian groups, but instead of a beautiful cake emerging from the oven, out popped a result no one wanted: a hard-as-a-rock cake that fell so flat, not even the dog would eat it.

We are convinced there is a recipe for discernment in Christian organizations, which, if followed, can regularly produce beautiful cakes. We have the assurance of success in this enterprise not because we are wonderful cooks, but because we have direct access to the work of the Master Chef, Jesus Christ our Lord. Christ has an even greater desire than we Christians do for Christian organizations to achieve their intended purpose in God's kingdom and in the world. He does not leave any of us to stumble around, wondering what ingredients should go into the cake. He assures us that the Holy Spirit is available for every committee meeting, every strategic planning session, and every business meeting, urging us toward God's highest and best purposes in God's work. The cake falls flat only when we randomly throw ingredients into the bowl, hoping that a culinary delight will emerge from the oven.

The authors struggled to find the most appropriate way to attach names and labels to God's guidance. Some believers prefer to use the name "God" to encompass all that they understand about the nature of God, including the Holy Spirit and Jesus Christ. Others prefer "Holy Spirit" language for God's work among Christians, since Jesus made it clear that the Holy Spirit was to be God's presence among humans until Christ's return. Still others prefer to speak of Jesus and Christ, or Jesus Christ, as the active agent of God in our midst, working to communicate, to guide, to correct, and to give confidence in the rightness of our corporate actions. We find ourselves using various names for God, knowing that none of them fully conveys the wondrous mystery of God at work in each moment of our lives. We trust that you will not feel distracted by the different names we use for God, but will focus on the reality of God's nurturing work. We know experientially that God— transcendent, immanent, and incarnational—is present as we gather to find *the way forward.*

While we think the concepts in this book can be applied to decision making in non-Christian groups, we have concentrated on the processes and dynamics particular to Christian groups. We are addressing those committed to Christ as Savior and Lord and whose organizations are deliberately and entirely devoted to doing God's work in the world. These organizations have many purposes: education, evangelism, community service, humanitarian relief, and building homes for the needy. They have in common a commitment to discern and to do God's work—and we believe that discovering God's mind is central to the process of healthy decision making.

Readers will soon realize that we are describing a form of decision making that does not include voting. They might expect us to describe our process as "consensus decision making," but we have chosen not to use that terminology. It has its place, especially among groups organized around something other than Christian principles. But we find that the term *consensus* too often describes a process of blending individual ideas without referring to God's leading. While we prefer the consensus process to authoritarian decision making and majority rule, it doesn't provide an adequate label for the process of dialogue with the living Christ in our midst.

Committees and other small decision-making groups commonly use consensus processes. This methodology involves listening to one another and agreeing informally on a course of action, rather than voting each time a decision is made. This can be done fairly easily in a committee of six to twelve—but what about a group of 40 or 60? Is it inevitable and appropriate that larger groups turn to voting as a means of reaching closure on discussions? Our experience tells us otherwise. And in this book we hope to show that even large Christian organizations can effectively discern God's leading and find ways forward without resorting to voting.

Each of us has talked with skeptics who support the theology of a Christian group seeking God's leading, but who say it doesn't generally work. They have agonized over the deadly combination of stubborn participants and ineffective leaders and have struggled with contentiousness, unresolved issues, endless delays, and fuzzy outcomes in Christian groups. While we acknowledge the existence of all these hazards, we intend to show that these problems do not come from making decisions in God's way. Rather, they come from our failure to make God an active partner in decision making. The remedy is not to resort to an even more human approach—voting—but to fix the problems in methodologies of listening to and following God's voice in our midst.

Some will recognize the authors' use of Quaker vocabulary and experiences, and indeed, the authors are Quakers. But the book is not written exclusively or even primarily for Quakers. The validity of these ideas and processes come from our grounding in God's truth, not from our origin within a particular Christian movement. We hope that all believers will find our vocabulary accessible and that people from many backgrounds will be able to adopt and adapt these methods. We have included a glossary toward the end of the book to clarify our use of terms and phrases.

The names at the beginning of each chapter identify the primary author(s) of those sections, but the three of us have fully collaborated with each other in the shape and content of the book. Words have flowed from the minds and hearts of one or the other of us, through our fingers and into our computers, but we have worked together to shape the words and ideas in the entire book. We trust that our different ways of thinking and expressing have strengthened the project.

To provide "real world" examples of group discernment, we will use three case studies to show how discernment principles can be implemented.

We are grateful to the many people whose thoughts have influenced our thinking and those who have helped strengthen the book. Those who have participated in workshops we have led on this subject have helped us find the energy and clarity to offer this work to a wider audience. We are particularly grateful for those who allowed us to interview them for the case studies in the book.

INTRODUCTION

Lon Fendall

To discern is to hear and understand God's voice as articulated by the Holy Spirit, resident within us. Discernment is a necessary precondition for faithfulness to God's leadings. This is as true for groups as it is for individuals, which means it is true for congregations and businesses that want to obey Christ. This book will flesh out the operating principles of discernment in the decision-making process of Christian groups.

Group discernment is an essential ingredient of anything that Christ's followers seek to do together. Even the smallest Bible study group or informal gathering makes decisions. That decision making carries with it the potential of strengthening the spiritual depth of each member of the group—but it also makes misunderstanding, division, and even the complete destruction of the group possible.

We invite you into an exploration of the ways God wants to enrich, instruct, and guide groups of believers called into common endeavors. The groups can range from informal to elaborately organized. They can be small or large. They can be made up of those who live close to one another or are widely scattered. These groups are part of the church, the body of Christ, so their members can expect to follow a constructive and consistent process of decision making. We choose to call

1

that process *discernment*, selecting a word with solid biblical grounding that also describes good contemporary decision making.

We can plunge into this particular meaning of discernment by looking at an example of decision making in the Old Testament.

An Exception to the Rule

King Jehoshaphat was a major exception to the general rule that the kings of ancient Judah and Israel were poor leaders and worse role models. Jehoshaphat "walked in the ways his father David had followed," unlike most other kings of that period (2 Chronicles 17:3-4). Scripture says "his heart was devoted to the ways of the LORD" and he destroyed the pagan places of worship (2 Chronicles 17:6).

Things went well during much of Jehoshaphat's reign. He instituted administrative reforms by appointing judges for each city. He undertook religious reforms by appointing priests to interpret God's law and to resolve disputes among the people. He even had a motto for all these reform measures: "May the LORD be with those who do well" (2 Chronicles 19:11).

But then Jehoshaphat ran into a potentially disastrous national security problem. Three of the Hebrews' formidable neighbors—the Moabites, Ammonites, and Meunites—formed an unholy alliance, moved into a threatening position, and declared war against the Hebrews. Intelligence officials came to the king with a terrifying report of the approaching army. Things did not look good for Judah! At this point Jehoshaphat turned to God and implemented an impressive discernment process that included the following concepts:

1. Turn to God First. God had predicted that future Hebrew kings would shift from trusting God to relying on military power. Jehoshaphat didn't make this mistake. While he took the nation's enemies seriously, he didn't rush to call a meeting of his generals to discuss appropriate military responses. Instead, he called for a national revival meeting and asked his people to come from every part of the nation to join in prayer and fasting. Jehoshaphat not only instituted this time of repentance and worship, but he also became its operational and spiritual leader. He covered several important points in his opening prayer (see 2 Chronicles 20:6-12):

- God rules over all and possesses all power.

- God would make it possible to conquer the enemy threat.

- It was God's problem to deal with the Moabites, for God had not allowed the Hebrews to conquer the Moabites in the past.

- The Hebrews had no power to resist the armies, so they had no plan of action that could succeed.

- They would turn their eyes to God for protection and guidance.

2. Be Attentive to God's Voice. Jehoshaphat got an intriguing and surprising answer to the first part of his prayer. God spoke through a prophet named Jahaziel, assuring the people that their prayers had been heard and they need not be afraid. While a battle would take place, God himself would fight for the Hebrew people; they would not have to lift a sword or string an arrow. At the same time, the Hebrews were not to stay at home during the defeat of their enemies; they were to go out to face the enemy and witness God's deliverance.

After receiving this inspiring message, Jehoshaphat continued to lead the people in worship. The fears of the people began to fade as they expressed their complete trust in God. No hint of timidity sullied their worship time. They exuberantly praised God, well into the night. And when time drew near to turn from worship to action, Jehoshaphat gave the benediction: "Have faith in the LORD your God and you will be upheld; have faith in his prophets and you will be successful" (2 Chronicles 20:20).

3. Courageously Carry Out God's Plan. Jehoshaphat was a decisive leader, not an autocrat. He consulted with the people before implementing the plans God had revealed to him. Put another way, the king and the people joined in a discernment process to be sure they understood and carried out God's plan for deliverance. Most kings would have responded to the crisis by organizing their armies and preparing their weapons. Amazingly, Jehoshaphat decided to hold a musical audition, for God directed him to select singers as his front line "soldiers" (2 Chronicles 20:21). Instead of looking for those skilled with swords and spears, the king called in the best sopranos, altos, tenors, and basses. Did the singers Jehoshaphat chose for the choir wish they had no musical talent when they discovered they were to perform at the head of the Hebrew army? We're not told. Gideon had previously used music in the miraculous defeat of a Midianite army, but in his case the music was instrumental, not vocal. His "soldiers" played trumpets and broke jars to reveal torches inside. God did not give Jehoshaphat such a dramatic plan. His Hebrew choral performers were simply to sing praises to God.

Throughout history God has delivered his people in a variety of ways when they fully trusted him. In this case, God defeated the enemies with absolutely no help from the Hebrews. God set ambushes among the enemies and they turned against each other and annihilated one another. When the Hebrews arrived, they found only a large number of corpses (2 Chronicles 20:22-24).

The account of Jehoshaphat teaches us several principles of discernment, which we will further investigate in the coming pages:

- The essence of discernment is hearing and obeying God's voice.

- Discernment is possible only if we look past the human dangers we face and focus on God's unlimited power.

- Discernment involves linking the attentiveness and obedience of the leaders with the people, so all agree in following God's direction.

- Discernment may lead to some unconventional ways of directing God's power to the "impossible" challenges being faced.

1

A NEW WAY TOWARD GROUP DISCERNMENT

Jan Wood and Lon Fendall

Jeremiah saw a time coming when discernment would come not only to leaders, priests, and teachers of Scripture, but to a much broader group. A time was coming when God would make a new covenant with God's followers, a new arrangement in human history:

> I will write it on their hearts. And I will be their God, and they shall be my people. And no longer shall each one teach his neighbor and each his brother, saying "Know the LORD," for they shall all know me, from the least of them to the greatest, declares the LORD. For I will forgive their iniquity, and I will remember their sins no more. (Jeremiah 31:33-34 ESV)

Just as Jeremiah predicted, the once-in-a-lifetime miracle of King Jehoshaphat later became an ongoing, water-into-wine wonder in the body of Christ, the church.

This prophecy began to be fulfilled with the coming of Jesus. Jesus came to show us in person what God is like. Jesus is the true reflection of God's heart, character, and perspective (see John 10:30; 14:8-11). Jesus brought the love and power of the Almighty into the lives of ordinary people. People were healed, released from unholy spirits, forgiven of their sins, and given a whole new lease on life. Jesus came to show God's plan for people to live and work together—the kingdom of God had come to earth, doing God's will here like it is done in heaven.

The kingdom is a here-and-now reality, with Jesus' followers as living witnesses to the reign of Christ in the middle of a world that does not recognize either its Creator or its King. Jesus lived and taught the kingdom of God, the gospel order. It clashed with the religious establishment. It threatened the powers, earthly and unearthly. The full fury of a world out of sync with its Creator unleashed its wrath on Jesus. And while he had the power to escape, he willingly entered into the fullness of death and evil.

But Godness could not stay dead. Jesus, the Son of God, could not stay entombed. The worst that could happen became the best thing that ever happened to this world. Jesus met and conquered everything that wars against the love of God. Jesus made a way through the rubble of each person's sins, addictions, and woundedness to freedom. Jesus rose to establish his rule and reign on this earth, *starting immediately.*

The incredible wonder is that he personally invites ordinary people like you and me to follow our King, Jesus, in establishing this wonderful good news order! The old ways of doing things are fulfilled and completed. This is a new adventure, a new way to do business on earth.

But no one has the power to live into this new system on his or her own. And so the final piece of the divine puzzle fell into place at Pentecost (see Acts 2). The very Spirit of God came to dwell in the hearts of Jesus' followers. The old ways began to pass away and everything was becoming new.

Amazing reordering happened inside of people and among people. They turned from their way of living to follow Jesus' kingship. Their burden of sins, addictions, and delusions fell away in the presence of Jesus as the gift and graces of the Holy Spirit empowered each believer. They surprised themselves as they began speaking in ways that reached across human barriers. Their fears melted away and courage took root. The newfound power that flowed through them amazed them all. They responded to one another with joy and enthusiasm in a new ordering of economic and social systems.

Traditions of private ownership blurred into an all-for-one-and-one-for-all heart. They put an end to the existence of the "haves" and "have-nots." They didn't think twice about crushing the walls of social, class, and ethnic distinctions; it felt only natural to open their homes and their lives to one another with glad and generous hearts. They offered exuberant praise to God, who had made all this possible, and their winsome new order caused their numbers to multiply quickly.

This same Pentecost spirit can become the mark of our living in the wonder of Jesus' reign. These same movements are to characterize our work, our play, our relationships, and our decision making. This is what Jesus saved us for—eternal partnership in the kingdom of God that starts right here on earth.

The Central Role of Discernment

Discernment is central to God's new order on the earth—and Jesus placed the Holy Spirit at the center of that teaching.

Jesus patiently comforted his disciples in anticipation of the sorrow they would feel at the time of his death. He said he would no longer be their daily companion and comforter. Instead, the Holy Spirit would become their permanent Comforter and Counselor, even more available to them than he had been. More than just giving them comfort, the Holy Spirit would assume Jesus' work of teaching. The Holy Spirit would be a true and knowable guide.

Understanding all of this, the apostle Paul clearly lays out the process by which believers will be able to discern God's truth and direction:

> …The Spirit searches all things, even the deep things of God. For who among men knows the thoughts of a man except the man's spirit within him? In the same way no one knows the thoughts of God except the Spirit of God. We have not received the spirit of the world but the Spirit who is from God, that we may understand what God has freely given us. This is what we speak, not in words taught us by human wisdom but in words taught by the Spirit, expressing spiritual truths in spiritual words. The man without the Spirit does not accept the things that come from the Spirit of God, for they are foolishness to him, and he cannot understand them, because they are spiritually discerned. The spiritual man makes judgments about all things, but he himself is not subject to any man's judgment: "For who has known the mind of the Lord that he may instruct him?" But we have the mind of Christ. (1 Corinthians 2:10-16)

In the normal scheme of things, God lies beyond human comprehension. Yet with remarkable generosity, God has chosen to share the very mind of Christ with every believer through the Holy Spirit. Amazingly, God gives us, as followers of Christ, the capacity to know God's heart and will through the capacity of discernment.

Group Discernment at Work in the Early Church

In the book of Acts, we see the Holy Spirit moving, shaping, and guiding—just as Jeremiah had foretold. The most impressive evidence of the Holy Spirit's presence among the people was not the absence of conflict, but the healthy and constructive ways of dealing with that conflict. The fifteenth chapter of Acts provides an impressive case study of the way Christ wants to lead the church through the Holy Spirit.

The group discernment process described in Acts 15 involved the core beliefs of two groups of people, both of whom were serious about being God's people.

Large numbers of people in Judea, the center of the Jewish world, had found excitement in their faith in Jesus as Savior and Lord and their experience with the cleansing and empowering presence of the Holy Spirit. Meanwhile, those in Antioch also felt thrilled with the excitement of their new experience of following Jesus and with the evidence of his indwelling Spirit. These disciples had no previous experience with the Jewish faith, so did not feel bound by Jewish law. They had come directly to Jesus without converting to Judaism and being circumcised. And so a dispute arose—not between pagans and Christians, or between unspiritual folks and spiritual. They were all brothers and sisters in Christ who had come out of very different faith backgrounds.

For the Judean believers, this was a simple issue. Since they themselves had come to faith in Christ out of a background of adherence to Jewish law, it was obvious to them that the Gentiles who found faith in Christ must also practice the fundamentals of Judaism. To them it was a seamless spiritual experience, not subject to individual picking and choosing. It was a clear matter of Scripture. The everlasting covenant of Abraham and Moses was not to be modified or reinterpreted.

Yet this fire of Pentecost continued to break out all over the known world. Peter saw God working among Cornelius and the Gentiles, just as God had worked in the upper room (see Acts 10). God wasn't waiting for anyone to become Jewish! The words of the Old Testament prophets were coming true before their very eyes. Surely the kingdom of God had come to earth in a new form!

Understandably, the flood of new converts unschooled in Jewish law and practice frightened the new Christians in Jerusalem. To deal with what they saw as heresy, they sent a "truth squad" to Antioch, where many were becoming followers of Christ under the preaching of Paul and Barnabas. They went with the urgent message that the new Gentile believers must be circumcised, thus accepting the Law and teachings God had given through Moses and the prophets.

So sure did the Judean truth squad feel about their position that they did not bother to check with Paul and Barnabas before pointing out what they felt were the errors of the Antioch believers. One can picture the Judean leaders holding a seminar on basic Jewish faith and practice. Paul and Barnabas walked in, sat down, and started taking notes. It took them only a few minutes to get the drift of the message from Jerusalem: Observe all the Jewish practices or don't pretend to be in right standing with God. Paul and Barnabas looked at each other with astonishment—and the people in the session began watching them, to see what they would say. Maybe the dialogue went something like this:

> "Excuse me," began Paul. "Did I understand you to say that everyone here must be circumcised and observe all the Jewish laws and practices? Didn't you hear that Peter learned in a vision that the old ways of separating the clean from the unclean and the chosen people from the outcasts no longer apply? And didn't you hear about Peter's visit to Caesarea to see Cornelius? I remember Peter telling me how he began his sermon at Caesarea: 'I now realize how true it is that God does not show favoritism, but accepts men from every nation who fear God and do what is right.' As Peter was preaching,

the Holy Spirit came on all the people—not just the Jews. Did
Peter instruct them that they must become Jews through
circumcision before their filling with the Holy Spirit could be
considered valid? Absolutely not! They were baptized as a
sign of their new faith in Christ and Peter placed no further
obligations on them. That seems clear enough to me. Doesn't
it seem clear to you, Barnabas?"

"Yes, Paul, and it seems to me to be significant that *Peter* was
the one who had this experience. Not only was he one of the
Lord's closest followers, but he has been the strongest leader
among the Christians in Jerusalem since Jesus' ascension. He
has shown us that we can't impose something on the Gentile
Christians that God is not asking of them. God is making a
new covenant with all of us."

"Well," responded Nathaniel, the leader of the truth squad, "I
think it's clear where you stand, but you're in great danger of
upsetting our ways of worshiping and being faithful to God.
How could Yahweh God, who was so clear in giving the
commandments and laws through Moses, suddenly change
direction? How could we turn our backs on all that our
forefathers believed in and died for? This is no small matter. I
think we will have to take the issue back to Jerusalem to be
settled."

"That suits us just fine, Nathaniel," Paul replied. "We're
confident that God is dealing with us in new ways these days.
Remember what Jesus said about new wine in old wineskins?
Give us a few days to discuss things here and to arrange for a
delegation to go to Jerusalem. We want to stop and see some
groups of believers between here and there. There are so
many exciting things happening among God's people these
days, we want to be ready to tell some of these stories in
Jerusalem and to encourage folks there with the good news of
God's mighty work!"

Focusing on God's Work and God's Ways

As the gathering in Jerusalem began, Paul and Barnabas focused on what they saw as most important. They reported to the church leaders the great things God was doing in the ministry in Antioch and in many other places. There could be reasonable disagreements about the program of the church, but there could be no argument about its mission.

God had called all of them to honor and glorify God, to open wide the doors of the kingdom so all believers could come in. No one should hang a sign over the church saying, "Only Jewish Christians need apply." When disputes arose in the work of the church, as they inevitably would, the starting point toward resolution would be returning to "square one" to determine what God is doing and what God is calling believers to do.

The world is familiar with decisions being made through hierarchy, control, power plays, and manipulation. The new way of the kingdom departs from those old ways of doing God's work. Authority no longer lies in money; class; or ethnic, religious, or national distinctions. In Christ there is no hierarchy of Jews, Greeks, men, women, slaves, or slave owners (Galatians 3:27-28). The elders of this birthing church remained committed to following the Holy Spirit rather than just plugging in their familiar way of doing religious business. They gathered to listen to one another and to God, who was speaking through the Holy Spirit.

Respecting Those with Whom We Disagree

The Pharisees, the self-appointed protectors of the status quo among the Jerusalem believers, were predictably the next to speak at the Jerusalem council. They jumped up and stated their case:

> "The Gentiles must be circumcised and required to obey the law of Moses," they insisted. When the spokesman for this position sat down, silence gripped the room.

> Paul happened to be sitting next to Peter and he leaned over and whispered, "Is that all they're going to say? I was ready for a two-hour summary of all the Holy Scriptures. I thought we would hear dire warnings about the dangers of compromising fundamental truths and requirements. I thought there would be some unpleasant comments about lowering the standards by letting all these 'foreigners' into the family of faith."

> Peter turned back to Paul and said quietly, "Actually, I'm not surprised that the Judaizers didn't try to defend their position. Basically, with the way God has been working among believers of all backgrounds these days, there's no way for them to defend their discrimination against Gentile believers. But, of course, it took a few visions and serious reordering of my own way of thinking before I came to my present position. Well, pray for me. I think it will soon be my time to speak."

> The room remained silent for some time. Those in the Antioch delegation felt tempted to express their anger and disappointment at the harsh position of the Judaizers. To their credit, they kept quiet. They showed love and respect toward the Jerusalem leaders, realizing that these believers were descended from many generations of family members for whom obeying the Jewish law was central to their spiritual identity.

The Acts passage describes "much discussion" regarding the ultimatum presented by the Judaizers. It does not describe shouting and quarreling, nor does it record attacks against the spirituality of the Jerusalem leaders. Instead, it appears the two sides spoke to each other with love and respect. They had begun to understand that mutual submission and respect are the foundation of relationships in the culture of God (Acts 10:44-47; Ephesians 4:1-3; 5:21). Humility and gentleness are the marks of a Spirit-filled citizen of the kingdom (Matthew 5:3-10; Galatians 5:22-23).

Powerful Use of Giftedness

After many comments flew back and forth, and allowing some time for reflection, Peter cleared his throat and stood up. "Brothers," he began.

What a freight of meaning was packed into the word *brother*! Peter considered the Jerusalem believers his brothers in Christ, with whom he happened to have a difference of opinion. What if he had begun, "My fellow believers, and all the rest of you who are here"? Had he done this, the meeting probably would have ended in division, just as it had begun.

The word *brother* had a special power to those participating in the meeting, especially to Paul. As Peter began speaking, Paul's memory flashed back to the day he sat blinded in Damascus, helpless and hopeless. A man he had never heard of came into the room, placed his hands on Saul, and said, "Brother Saul." That greeting had said it all—and Peter had captured the same depth of compassion with one word.

Peter continued calmly, but became more forceful as he progressed. By giving the gift of the Holy Spirit freely to all who responded in faith—and not placing on them any advance requirements, such as circumcision—God had settled the matter. Did God withhold the Holy Spirit until people underwent the rite? No. So what was there to discuss?

Before he finished, Peter couldn't resist exposing the shallow spirituality of some of the Judaizers. They were defending a system of laws and requirements that *none* of them had been able to fully carry out. Did they not recall that Jesus had offered them a new, easy-to-carry kind of yoke? Christ removed the legalism and offered in its place the freedom of loving service.

Peter ended with a call to his fellow Jerusalem leaders to freely accept God's gift of grace through Jesus Christ, who had fulfilled and completed the Jewish law.

Listening in Silence

One indication of Peter's effectiveness in the meeting was the response. Instead of the assembly hall erupting in shouting and arguments, the crowd became silent again. Not even the most zealous Pharisees in the group could question what Peter had said.

Something new was clearly happening! They needed time to process it. Over in one corner, one of the Jerusalem leaders stood to his feet, but soon sat down. Those near him heard him recite one of the verses from the Proverbs, "Even a fool is thought wise if he keeps silent, and discerning if he holds his tongue" (Proverbs 17:28).

Refocusing on Faithfulness to God's Mission

If Paul and Barnabas had urged the council to make a hasty decision, it wouldn't have worked. Instead, they offered the best possible arguments, which weren't really arguments at all. They told stories, one after another. They used names. They talked about specific places and situations, some of them from their trip from Antioch to Jerusalem.

In each case, the point of the story was unmistakable: God was at work among those who put their trust in God. The miraculous things that were happening could be explained only as the work of God—God's grace being poured out on people, without regard to their religious and ethnic backgrounds. The mission of the church, they said, was to welcome people into God's kingdom.

> "The Gentiles as well as the Jews are responding to the Holy Spirit's work in great numbers," Paul said. "Who are we to block the central mission of the church and the heart of Christ?"

Giving Voice to God's Answer

One could suppose that another time of silent waiting and listening took place after Paul and Barnabas finished. Would Peter be the next to speak? Would one of the Judaizers try to rescue their weak case?

No, it was one of Peter's fellow apostles, James, who rose to his feet and presented God's message to the group. He began once again with that powerful word of acceptance, understanding, and love: *brothers*. He said that clearly God was calling out from among the Gentiles a people who would be God's own. The Jews had indeed been God's chosen ones, but had rarely acted that way. They thought their genealogy would assure their place in God's kingdom. Now they were to understand the covenant in a new way—not restricted to those born as Jews, but open to all those who would remain faithful to God.

James offered a quote from the prophet Amos, looking ahead to the day when it would be understood that God would gladly claim people from every nation and background. At the same time, James made it clear that there was to be no "cheap grace" for the Gentile believers. They were to uphold a high standard of personal purity. They were to separate themselves from their idolatrous culture, especially by not eating meat offered to idols. They were to live lives of sexual purity—at a time when idolatry and immoral behavior were closely linked.

Documenting the Decision and the Follow-Up Steps

One can see from the context that the council members readily accepted the Holy Spirit's solution. Something very compelling and compassionate about the plan James proposed swayed them, along with the manner in which he presented it. The attention shifted almost immediately from the problem to the solution.

Having come to a decision, they must take the important step of putting it in writing. Someone at the meeting with the gift of expression and discernment prepared a letter for the Antioch believers. The letter began with an apology for the trouble caused by the Judaizers. The heart of the letter forcefully stated that the Holy Spirit had made the decision, with the full agreement and cooperation of those present.

There is something wonderful about the kind of partnership with the Holy Spirit described in Acts 15:28: "It seemed good to the Holy Spirit and to us not to burden you." It pleased the Holy Spirit. It pleased the council members. The attention shifted to an effective means of communicating the outcome of the meeting. No one had any doubt about the strength of the support behind the decision to bring an end to the circumcision requirement for Gentile believers. The Antioch believers also had to know the importance of the new Gentile believers living godly, holy lives. To communicate the "between-the-lines" feelings of the letter, the council appointed Judas and

Silas to personally carry the letter to Antioch and to express the warmth of love and acceptance that lay at the heart of the council's decision.

Celebrating the Work of God's Spirit

What a great choice the council made in their selection of goodwill ambassadors! Judas and Silas not only carried the letter to the folks at Antioch and answered their questions, they encouraged and strengthened them as well. The outreach to Gentiles almost stopped when some insisted that the faith and practice of believers remain as it always had. No doubt the word had gone out among other groups of believers that this was a crucial "test case" that could go in the direction of either stifling evangelism or opening the doors to receiving the believing Gentiles. Perhaps folks gathered at Antioch from other locations, ready to carry the good (or bad) news to other places.

Did believers say "amen" as a way to thank God for what transpired? I don't know. Did they say, "Yippee" (or its equivalent in Greek) and throw their hats in the air? Maybe. Did they break out into songs of praise to God, the great Welcomer of the faithful and the great Reconciler of people? We think so.

Whatever the case, this powerful passage in Acts provides us with several crucial principles of discernment, which we will unpack in chapters to come:

- Intense conflict is an invitation to turn to God, who wants to lead us forward into restored relationships and into new organizational processes.

- Discernment requires that we focus and refocus on what God is doing, rather than on what we think should be done.

- Discernment requires respectful listening to others who have joined us in seeking God's voice.

- Discernment requires that each person faithfully offer up his or her own giftedness.

- Discernment requires honesty and candor about deep feelings.

- Discernment should include times of silent listening to God's voice.

- Discernment means being open to God saying something different from what we expected.

2

CULTIVATING FOUNDATIONAL DISCERNMENT SKILLS

Bruce Bishop

Before we can shed light on the ways group discernment operates, we must first look closely at how individuals hear God.

Discernment is a process by which the hunger to know God becomes reality. It is at the core of the spiritual journey and central to our relationship with God and our commitment to be Christ-followers. Discernment is the dialogue between us and the living Christ, the Holy Spirit who is here to "teach [us] all things and...remind [us] of everything" Christ taught us (John 14:26).

We believe that God speaks with us all the time, whispering in our ears, nudging our emotions, stirring our senses, and drawing us to the preferred path. Even now, as you read these words, God may be stirring within you, calling, opening, and speaking to you. God desires to be your partner, to journey through life with you.

Both God and humans seek the reality of this dialogue and companionship. Spiritual discernment is the process of learning the language and the process of this relationship. For some, it is a spiritual gift that comes easily and that has always been a part of their awareness. But it is also an art and a skill that can be developed. The art of discernment is learning to first be attentive, and then to sift through the many spirits vying for our attention to hear the One True Spirit.

Limitations of Language and Temperament

It is important to remember that human language has limitations. When we speak of "hearing" God or of God "speaking" with us, we use words that imply physical hearing. Most often, however, God communicates with us without words that we hear with our physical ears. The infinite God has an unlimited number of ways to communicate with us. We need to expand the language of "speaking" and "hearing" to include the wide diversity of God's many means of communication.

It is important and exciting to discover God's unique processes for communicating with each of us. What works well for the person next to you, for your mother or your pastor, may not work for you. Discovering your style of communication with Christ may release you from the guilt and frustration you've carried for years over not hearing God in the "normal" ways. It may help you celebrate who you are as a unique creation. It will surely help you become better able to discern God's mind and desires for your life.

God Is on Our Side

God *wants* us to hear the voice of the Divine. God says: "Listen! I am standing and knocking at your door. If you hear my voice and open the door, I will come in and we will eat together" (Revelation 3:20 CEV). James 4 reminds us that as we "draw near to God," God will respond to our movement and come near to us, as well.

Christ will not play hide-and-seek with us, speaking randomly, switching methods of communication with us just to stay out of reach. God doesn't throw a stone into a bush to distract us while running in the opposite direction. No, God *desires* to be heard. God *longs* to be in a partnership with us and to walk hand-in-hand with us through life. "Whether you turn to the right or to the left, you will hear a voice saying, 'This is the road! Now follow it'" (Isaiah 30:21 CEV).

Often we approach discernment as though it were a task forced upon God. So often we seem to think of the process as adversarial, as if we had to sneak up on Christ to catch him and then convince him to speak. But Christ is no adversary. He is Friend and Beloved. God *wants* us to hear. God comes all the way to us so that we can hear and know. And because of this, God often communicates with us in consistent ways that eventually create patterns that are both increasingly recognizable and unique to our temperaments.

This chapter is about learning to recognize the patterns God has been using in our lives. As John 10:4 states it: "His sheep follow him because they know his voice." We really can become familiar with God's means of communication with us.

Developing a Discernment Portfolio

By developing our skills to recognize the movement of God in our lives, we find the Spirit's patterns of communication becoming more familiar to us, allowing us to discern God's leading more quickly and confidently. We can assemble these patterns into what we might call a "Discernment Portfolio."

We normally use the word *portfolio* in reference to a collection of drawings, photography, or some other representation of a person's creative ability. A portfolio serves as a record of accomplishments that demonstrates a person's skills—useful for when he or she goes for a job interview or applies to an educational program. Your discernment portfolio is a collection of the signs and experiences that let you know when God seems to be stirring within you. You can keep these signals close in your memory, or even write them down, to be able to refer to them (or remain open to them) when listening for the voice of God.

As you're assembling your portfolio, be open to new and creative ways God might communicate. God sometimes communicates in a way that doesn't fit the patterns you've come to recognize. The possibility of that happening might make you wary about having confidence in certain patterns of communications—but when the donkey talks, we know it's God!

The Old Testament prophet Balaam heard that unusual voice when he didn't listen to God speaking in ways that had become familiar to him (see Numbers 22). God startled him to attention by speaking through Balaam's donkey. And Balaam had no doubt that he was hearing the voice of God!

These "out-of-left-field" ways of communicating are usually clear and stand out as unusual. We *know* that something is up. So don't worry that creating a discernment portfolio might rule out the possibility of your catching a unique communication from God. Instead, focus on the common, everyday ways God communicates in your life—over and over again—realizing that the unusual voices will stand out and present themselves as clearly authentic.

Being Attentive

If God is constantly stirring within us, reaching out every day to communicate and journey with us, then why do we rarely hear this communication? Some might think that barriers within themselves—like sin or something defective—are to blame. But what barrier could prove too strong for God? Psalm 139 makes it clear that there is no place we can go, no action we can perform, that will cause God to be inaccessible to us.

More likely, our lack of hearing God has to do with our lack of focus and attention.

Rather than occasionally dipping into the presence of God, we need to learn to allow ourselves to sink deeply into that awesome presence. God wants us to slow down and spend more time surrounded by God's presence. We need to release the distractions of our own agendas and our own desires, allowing ourselves to be surrounded by, supported by— completely immersed in—the presence of God. This is not necessarily a call to be less busy, but rather, less distracted. You can spend the day sitting on your couch and still not settle into the presence of God. Conversely, you can go about the demands of your day while still cultivating your attentiveness to the presence of God.

Learning to listen to the Spirit is one of the fundamental disciplines of the followers of Christ, and it precedes the ability to discern. We are called to journey through our lives with Christ, as did his disciples, receiving constant teaching, fellowship, and companionship. Throughout Scripture, listening to God is presented as a foundational discipline.

Are you committed to creating space in your life to be in the presence of God—to sit at Christ's feet, like Mary, and simply *listen* (see Luke 10:38-42)? That comes first in developing the art of discernment. By *art* I mean that there is no list of easy steps that pertain to everyone. Learning to dialogue with Christ is the same sort of art form as an intimate friendship. It takes time to develop it and is unique to the personalities involved.

Frank Laubach, the great literacy advocate and missionary, spoke of his "Game with Minutes" in which he would take an hour each day and see how many of those sixty minutes he could remain conscious of God's presence.[1] Perhaps each time you look at your watch, you could use that action as a trigger to turn your attention to God; or use the watch's hourly beep to bring you back to an awareness that God is present in the mundane details of your day. As you develop that habit, deepen it by trying to turn your focus to God on the half hour as well, and then the quarter hour.

Thomas Kelly wrote about this focus by using the term *simultaneity.* "There is a way of ordering our mental life on more than one level at once," he wrote. "On one level we may be thinking, discussing, seeing, calculating, meeting all the demands of external affairs. But deep within, behind the scenes, at a profounder level, we may also be in prayer and adoration, song and worship and a gentle receptiveness to divine breathings."[2]

Laubach and Kelly, as well as Brother Lawrence, Jean Pierre de Caussade, and many other godly men and women have written about the disciplines that deepened their attentiveness to God. All of them have given us insights that apply directly to discernment.

To settle into a holy awareness of God's presence does not require us to quit doing what we are doing, but to discipline ourselves to focus on God in the midst of our daily living and working. While it may require intentionality to practice living fully in the presence of God, it is also very natural. It is very similar to being in love.

When we are in love, we are constantly aware of our beloved, regardless of what we are doing or where we are. We have tuned in to the opinions, moods, wants, and needs of that special one. We have a natural consciousness of him or her that rises from a heart of love and delight. And so it is with our relationship with God. It is not hard to be aware of someone who adores us. It is not difficult to want to know what our beloved is thinking and feeling. It isn't a chore to share our life with a God who is totally wonderful.

So learning to listen—being attentive to the Spirit—is one of the primary disciplines and joys of the Christ-follower. We must learn to be a discerning people. We can't just swallow the cultural values that surround us. We can't assume that everything labeled as *Christian* contains or expresses truth, nor can we abdicate our personal responsibility to be in a genuine relationship with God. Our pastor or friend cannot be an intermediary between Christ and us. Jesus is alive and calling us, and if we don't pursue his invitation, we may find we called him "Lord" but never really knew him (Matthew 7:23).

The Three Channels Through Which We See God

Individual discernment comes from processing the leadings and nudgings we receive from three sources: the Bible, our faith community, and our direct listening to God.

Africans would use the metaphor of three large stones that support a cooking pot over an open fire. We in the north might think of a three-legged stool, with all of its legs supporting us. A stool cannot remain upright with just one or two legs. The same is true with spiritual discernment. In any experience of looking for God's leading (and *especially while* we are just beginning), we must always check our personal leadings, our understanding of Scripture, and our experience of the faith community. God's truth lies at the intersection of these three elements. If any one of the three does not support the others, then we have not completed the work of discernment.

Our faith community may be a combination of our church, a small group, or an assortment of individuals we respect spiritually. It may be a group brought together for discernment, or it may be our church's meeting for business. These are all valid components of the body of Christ. We can also access our faith community through historical writings, devotional classics, and the history of the church. We do not stand isolated in this period of time, but share the experience of being Christ-followers with people throughout the ages. If we listen only to the leadings of our faith community and do not seek confirmation from the broad truths of Scripture and our personal hearing of God's voice, however, we can be led into falsehood. This is how cults come into being.

The teachings of Scripture are crucial for maintaining balance and discovering God's voice. For example, the fruit of the Spirit should always be evident in any leading of God. God has spoken clearly through these teachings and will not contradict them. Still, one look at Christianity in both the past and the present reveals that personal bias can be introduced into biblical interpretation and can be supported through the use of isolated texts. The Ephesians 6:5 admonition to slaves to respect their masters, for example, was used for many centuries to justify the selling and keeping of slaves. A broader reading of the themes of Scripture, however, upholds the imperative to treat each human with dignity and not to treat anyone as property. Becoming aware of the broad themes of Scripture that point to the character of God and to God's desires for humanity will help us avoid an abuse of these teachings.

And without these balancing factors in our lives, simply following our personal leadings can draw us into a relativism that knows *no* truth. Personal leanings can simply perpetuate a familiar culture or personal experience. We may believe, for example, that violence is the way to settle problems. But this notion comes from our culture, not from the teachings of Jesus. Similarly, we might feel God calling us to do exactly what we most wish for (or what we most deeply fear). Looking for the intersection with the other two avenues of God's communication will help us avoid falling prey to our humanness or to mere cultural prejudices.

Discernment Portfolio Contents

Since we tend to neglect our personal experience of God's voice more than any other channel of hearing from God, the remainder of this chapter will focus on that idea. In the section that follows, we will encourage you to prayerfully consider the ways God stirs different temperaments.

Each temperament naturally responds to different elements from the list. This is the way we were created. As you read through them, don't breeze over or dismiss any of the elements. It may be that God wants to use them in your life—or has before, and you just haven't had the words to label them. As you consider times that you have experienced God's leading, some of these will connect with your experience. These are the avenues of communication that belong in your personal discernment portfolio.

1. Scripture. The Bible is filled with insights, challenges, truth, stories that connect or prod, and recurring themes that guide us. For each of us, Scripture needs to be an active part of our discernment process. For some of us, it will be a primary way that God gets our attention, bringing verses to mind or guiding us to specific passages while reading.

2. The Faith Community. From other believers we receive feedback, response, advice, words of affirmation, histories, challenges, prophetic leadings, and insights. Again, each of us must have these relationships. Some of us will find God's voice quite regularly in such relationships.

3. Circumstances. We often refer to "open and closed doors" when we talk about God's leadings, believing God is at work in guiding us through the details of our life experiences. This is one means God uses to speak to us, and for some of us, it might become a primary means—one of our portfolio items.

But be careful to exercise your discernment skills in evaluating circumstances. Just because something seems "easy" or available doesn't mean God has opened a door for you. And something that feels difficult and requires a lot of effort isn't necessarily a door you're "forcing open" that God wants shut. Circumstances can contribute to our discernment process, but we should balance them with several other indicators of God's direction.

4. Conceptual Understandings. The Holy Spirit can speak to us through our reasoning skills and beliefs. Perhaps you are guided more by reason than by emotions. God can use that aspect of your temperament. Look carefully at your assumptions, at your metaphors and beliefs. Be aware of theological, political, and psychological thoughts and concepts that bear on the situation or have weight in your life. Hold each of these up to the light of Christ and allow that light to penetrate and clarify them.

Perhaps some of your conceptual understandings need to be tweaked to become more in line with the truth of God's character. When they are aligned with God's own desires and understandings, they can be avenues of hearing God's voice. These are "left-brain" ways of hearing from God.

5. Emotions. Like circumstances, our emotions can become windows into God's will. God may speak through joy, desire, sorrow, attraction, repulsion, anxiety, fear, longing, anger, pain, freedom, surprise, and peace. Each of these indicates something about God's leadings, telling us whether we are getting closer to or further from God's desire.

The distinct absence of emotion can also signal God's stirring. If you normally experience emotions in certain situations and are not experiencing them in this case, this may point to what God is doing or saying in that moment. What is different? Why do you feel differently? Or feel nothing at all? In such situations, take the time for prayerful consideration.

6. Imagery. Many people are naturally visual, finding concepts and leadings through imagery rather than abstractions or words. For such "right-brain" people, it is important to be aware of the ways images, fantasies, metaphors, flights of imagination, daydreams, colors, art, nature, and music impact and speak to you. Also consider the distinct absence of these things if they are normally present. Has God used any of these in the past to get your attention or communicate truth to you?

7. Intentions. We each have a will—a part of our self that draws us toward certain decisions and holds us to them, a part of us that helps us follow through on our commitments. God can use our will. Be aware of your levels of willingness, the choices before you, the aspirations that tantalize, the depth of convictions, any sense of drawing that you feel. Also be aware of the distinct absence of intentions.

8. Supernatural Interventions. Scripture is full of stories of God approaching humans through supernatural means, such as dreams, angels, and prophetic visions. The Israelites came to expect such encounters. Western Christians have downplayed those expectations, but that doesn't change the character and creativity of God. Dreams that seem to carry more weight or impact may well express God's voice. "Entertained strangers" (Hebrews 13:2) may potentially be angels bringing a message. Yes, we might feel uncomfortable with this category. But God has used these supernatural interventions in the past and has not indicated they have become obsolete. Our discomfort is good if it urges us to seek confirmation from the other sources of God's leading. But we shouldn't get so locked into rational thinking as to deny God this avenue of leading us.

9. Physical Sensations. Many of us feel wary of experiencing God physically. Yet haven't we sometimes felt a churning in our stomachs as God spoke to us? Or perhaps a sense of warmth when God comforted us? God intentionally created our bodies to house our spirits as well as God's indwelling Spirit (see 1 Corinthians 6:19). So it seems logical that God would have created our bodies so that they would respond to the stirrings of our spirits and to the direct touch of God's presence.

In his book *The Spirit of the Disciplines*,[3] Dallas Willard makes a strong case for the spiritual *necessity* of our bodies— that our spirits are *meant* to be contained in physical vessels. He suggests that, like the classic spiritual disciplines, the things we do physically impact our spirits.

So, as you consider God's movement and leadership in your life, be aware of physical sensations, such as cold, heat, prickliness, knots in the stomach, muscles relaxing or tightening, goosebumps, stillness, a change in breathing, and body posture. Once again, a distinct lack of physical sensation can also be a signal that God is active.

Another way God might use our bodies is to prompt us to move *while* we pray. Perhaps putting your body in motion by taking a walk or dancing will help your mind and spirit become clearer. Exercise might calm your spirit or discipline your mind or draw your attention to some specific manifestation of the still, small voice of God. Kneeling or lying prostrate on the floor might help you express your spirit.

10. The Unexpected. There is no way we can know the complete mind of Christ or the limits of his creativity. Sometimes the donkey will speak. Sometimes we experience inward sighs too deep for words, or interior movements that we can sense but can't describe. Perhaps we sense an intellectual or physical opening, or a stirring that can't be put into words.

Explore on Your Own

Becoming aware of the patterns God uses to get your attention and communicate with you will help you to differentiate between God's voice and the voice of the culture. We have looked at a few of the more common ways God approaches humanity, but these ways are far from constituting an exhaustive list.

You have the joyful task of exploring your unique relationship with God and uncovering your own discernment portfolio. And as you do, may you echo the young Samuel's words as he too learned to discern God's voice: "Speak, LORD, for your servant is listening" (1 Samuel 3:9).

THE INDIVIDUAL'S ROLE
IN GROUP DISCERNMENT

Lon Fendall

Becoming aware of God's movement and hearing God's voice is foundational for each person participating in group discernment and decision making. While the last chapter described ways to develop our personal discernment processes, this chapter will examine the individual's place in the group discernment process.

The individual's role is distinct from submitting to hierarchy or voting in a democracy. Rather, that role is to listen to God's voice and to express that leading in ways that help the group reach clearness about the way forward for the group.

Worship, the Individual's Preparation for Discernment

One day Jesus faced an important step in his ministry. He had to discern who would become part of his small group of co-workers, the ones to whom he would entrust the message of the good news.

Early in the morning Jesus went out to pray about the issue (Luke 4:42; 6:12). He knew he was about to pick a very important group of followers and future leaders, all of them gifted-but-weak human beings with a vital mission ahead of them. Would it be worth investing time in men who would not understand much of his teaching and who would fail him at crucial points? That was the burden Jesus laid before the Father in the sleepy hours before others woke up, in a place where no one would disturb him.

For us, as for Jesus, worship is inseparable from discernment. Those who desire to effectively participate in group discernment will be able to do so only if they have nurtured their individual discernment skills, are aligning with God's heart, and with purposeful prayer have entered as a group into each discernment challenge. A quick devotional or opening prayer most likely will not fully align our hearts with God's. Take the time needed for meaningful worship. The key component of worship as preparation for group discernment is to learn to listen to God:

> "Now then, my sons, listen to me; blessed are those who keep my ways. Listen to my instruction and be wise; do not ignore it. Blessed is the man who listens to me, watching daily at my doors, waiting at my doorway." (Proverbs 8:32-34)

Homework in Preparation for Discernment

Homework is the next important step in listening to God. There may be important information that will guide the group's listening process.

For example, one might find a Web site with helpful background information about a person under consideration for an upcoming speaking engagement. One might need to make a phone call to seek some information that would fill in missing pieces concerning some issue facing the group. Doing homework certainly means reading the information distributed by the clerk. Nothing is more frustrating than leading a group toward a decision and finding that some of the participants have not read the agenda or the detailed recommendations circulated in advance of the meeting.

Doing homework might mean confessing the ways we have hurt other people. By hurting others we may hinder our participation in group discernment. In the Sermon on the Mount, Jesus instructed us to abandon any attempt to participate in worship if we have not dealt with things we have done that have hurt our brothers and sisters. Reconciliation and confession remove the roadblocks to worship (Matthew 5:24). Sometimes confession may be personal—recognizing our own biases and blind spots and laying them on the altar so we do not hinder our discernment.

Doing homework might also mean exploring ways to reconcile opposing viewpoints. A very practical form of peacemaking involves talking with those who disagree about an important question. Through talking with people we can begin to see possibilities that remained hidden when the group first discussed the issue. We can ask things such as, "What if we were to do this? How would that make us feel?" In an unthreatening way we can say to others, "I'm not sure I understood what you meant when you expressed your point of view in the last business meeting." Or we can ask, "Could you explain to me why you think the way you do?" We can affirm our love and respect for people with whom we disagree, not letting our differences of opinion get detoured into expressions of negative feelings toward the person. We can affirm our trust that God will direct us into a place of clarity about a decision, even when it seems unlikely we will get past the differences that divide us.

Supportive Prayer During Decision Making

Thomas Kelly talks about the flow of prayerful listening to God through those who have been praying prior to the meeting and carry forward that unceasing prayer during the meeting for business:

> *Some* individuals need already, upon entering the meeting, to be gathered deep in the spirit of worship. There must be some kindled hearts when the meeting begins. In them, and from them, begins the *work* of worship. The spiritual devotion of a few persons, silently deep in active adoration, is needed to kindle the rest, to help those others who enter the service with tangled, harried, distraught thoughts to be melted and quieted and released and made pliant, ready for the work of God and His Real Presence.[1]

One of my favorite verses as a child was 1 Thessalonians 5:17 (KJV), "Pray without ceasing." It was not a favorite because I had grasped its deep meaning, but because it was short. If a Sunday school teacher expressed a willingness to give a reward for memorizing a verse—no matter how long—this one seemed like a good choice.

Praying during a business meeting is one way of praying without ceasing. Perhaps the continuous prayer might be "thy will be done" or "we trust you" as we take our breaths. Perhaps it is the prayer of beaming God's love to all the participants. Perhaps it is holding a mental image of Jesus in the midst of the meeting.

Since effectiveness in group discernment requires that we speak only occasionally, we will have plenty of opportunities to pray. While we listen attentively to others speak, we can simultaneously listen to God. At their best, the words of others will be God's words. Listening to these words is part of our prayer.

We can hear the pain behind a person's words and we can pray that Jesus will heal that pain. We can hear the anger in someone's voice and we can ask Jesus if our actions had a part in producing that anger.

I've learned that I can see the evidence of the feelings I had during a business meeting by looking at my notes or my doodles. Pages full of messy scrawling probably mean that I found the meeting difficult. Not knowing how to express those emotions, I use my paper as the recipient of my frustrations. Doodling might be a form of prayer, I suppose. But it may also mean that I need to shift from fretting to expressing prayers of confession for feeling upset with other speakers. It might be better to stop looking at the strange designs my pencil creates and focus all my attention on others in the meeting, praying specifically for them as they struggle with personal and organizational issues.

Listening: The Essential Skill for Decision Making

Those who facilitate workshops on effective group process often talk about "active listening"—the skill of hearing and processing the ideas behind another person's words. When someone does not understand the ideas being conveyed, the active listener asks questions such as, "I'm not sure I understand what you mean by...?" or "Could you tell me more about your feelings about...?" or "Do I hear you saying that...?" Even if we think we know what a person means, it helps to check.

Sometimes the active listener paraphrases the person's message and "plays it back" to him or her, to make sure both parties understand clearly. In that process, the active listener often inserts some descriptors of the person's feelings, since most of us do not feel comfortable naming our feelings when we feel agitated. In that naming process, we must remain alert to indications that we have used inaccurate labels and so ask the first party to make corrections. We can also simply name what we see, saying: "I notice that your voice quavered when you said this. Would you like to tell us more of what you are feeling?" It's important to accurately understand the emotions as well as the words.

While these active-listening skills are necessary in group discernment, they are not sufficient. We need to look more deeply for the "value added" that comes from listening to the Holy Spirit speaking through others.

We find a fascinating scriptural example of Holy Spirit–focused active listening in the book of Judges. The Hebrews had let themselves get into a terrible situation—ignoring God's commandments and suffering the consequences during a period of Midianite oppression. Gideon was threshing his crop of wheat while hiding in a winepress, hoping the Midianites wouldn't find him and steal the provisions he needed for his family.

An angel came to Gideon and addressed him as "mighty warrior." "The LORD is with you, mighty warrior," the angel said (Judges 6:12). Gideon must have considered the greeting a joke, since he felt like a coward for hiding from the enemy and since he had no thought of facing the Midianites in battle. The conversation could have ended there, like someone hanging up on a telemarketer. But Gideon was a good listener. When the message didn't fit the situation, he asked for clarification. How could God be with his people if they had absolutely no evidence of God's mighty hand at work? This may seem like arguing, but Gideon was actually seeking information, trying to reconcile the angel's pronouncement with the reality he was experiencing.

Gideon continued with his active listening, seeking to understand the parts of God's message that clashed with his own perception of reality. The angel presented God's call to Gideon to deliver the Hebrews. But again Gideon had a question: How could he be the leader when he was the weakest family member in the weakest Hebrew clan? Gideon needed some proof that it was almighty God speaking through the angel. After all, the angel probably didn't have wings like those we see in children's Sunday school materials. He looked like a man, and Gideon wanted to be sure he was hearing God's voice, not hallucinating after a hard day of threshing grain.

God accepted Gideon's honest desire for confirmation and provided three miracles: God sent fire to consume some meat and bread; he sent moisture to drench some dry wool; then he kept some other wool dry when the ground around it became wet with dew. God did some amazing things through Gideon because Gideon was an excellent listener who determined to hear God's voice through the words of the angel and the miraculous events (see Judges 6—7).

Earlier we talked about the importance of constant prayer during a group discernment process. A group discernment process is essentially a process of listening carefully to God. And isn't that what prayer is, after all? Not pouring out a bunch of words, asking God for all sorts of things. It is tuning out the distractions, including the words that do not convey God's truth. We treat those words as chaff, knowing there is no threshing without chaff. But we find grains of wheat hidden in the chaff! Those grains are God's words that we can recognize only if we are attentive.

As we listen for God's voice, we do not at the same time compose our next words, as though we needed to rebut our opponent's statements in a debate. We don't need to argue with others involved in the discernment process, for discernment is not the same as a debate. We simply need to listen for God's truth in what others are saying, even when it appears hidden among some unhelpful words. Some have used the phrase "listening in tongues" for this process. The people at Pentecost heard other languages as though they were their own. Careful listening means hearing what people intend to say and discerning the thoughts behind the words, not hearing only the words actually spoken.

The effective clerk will insist that the group take some time between the statements to listen to God. Participants must support the clerk in this effort by waiting until the words of others have soaked in. Then and only then should participants switch from listening to speaking. And that speaking should flow directly from their listening to God.

THE LISTENING PROCESS IN LAYING DOWN A VALUED CHURCH MINISTRY

This first case study emphasizes the listening processes central to a church's decision on a difficult issue.

It's easier to start a church ministry than to end one. After 30 years of operating a day care program, some members of a church in Seattle felt that the ministry and the church had become inseparable. Others felt that it was time to consider laying down this outreach because the gifts, ministry, and energies of the church had changed over time. Still others felt concerned about issues of liability and the need for major improvements in the building if the program was to be continued.

In short, this was a heavy decision. No one could accuse the church of taking the issue lightly. Seven months would pass before the church had completely resolved the issue. During those months, the church held seven general business meetings devoted partly or entirely to the issue. Additionally, about 20 other meetings of various types took place—listening meetings, committee meetings, working group meetings, administrative committee meetings, and staff meetings.

The members of the church remained remarkably determined to discern God's leading about the future of their day care program—and in the process to strengthen, not weaken, their church. The process went through three distinct phases: a decision, a crisis, and then the reconsideration that led to a new decision.

The first phase occurred during the first three weeks of the process. The participants in a business meeting decided it was important to continue the day care ministry and to take the necessary steps to assure it had strong leadership and solid financial backing. Many months and many meetings later, the same members united around the opposite decision. They found the whole process to be exhausting in some ways and exhilarating in others. They looked back and saw that God had been at work, drawing people beyond the apparent clarity of that first stage of the process to solid agreement over the ultimate decision to end the church's involvement with childcare.

The process of reaching one decision, then reversing it without in any way letting go of the commitment to hear and do God's will, fascinated us as authors. To gather the memories and impressions of this discernment process, Bruce Bishop facilitated a meeting of those who had participated in the decision. This process of reflection became one more step in confirming the rightness of the decision. It allowed some key people to remember and analyze the positive results of hearing and obeying God's voice.

Should the Program Continue?

No one in the church had been looking for a decision that would enhance the church's skills in group discernment. The decision found them.

It started with an announcement that the day care director had resigned. That by itself was not a cause for panic, for the director had given three months notice—plenty of time to find a replacement. While the pastor had no interest in stirring up trouble, she sensed an opportune time to address some questions about organizational structure, finances, facilities, and curriculum. Even though she did not propose that the church discontinue the day care program, she felt the time had come for a thorough evaluation process and that this process should examine termination as one option.

Some in that first business meeting agreed that all options should be considered, but they could not see themselves *ever* supporting the closure of the day care program or its relocation. They saw it as a valuable ministry to families and felt that strengthening families was one of the most important things the church could be doing. They knew it had taken a lot of the church leaders' energy, but they also knew the children were being cared for in a safe place, were being loved, and were receiving solid Christian teaching. They realized that the church shouldered burdens in having children in the building all week, but they felt the program's financial contributions adequately covered those costs.

Others in the church felt pleased with the raising of hard questions and agreed that the change in the director position provided the ideal time to do it. They weren't lobbying for hastily pulling the plug, but they wanted the church to answer the pastor's questions. They wondered what would happen to the church if the program's leaders were one day charged with negligence in the children's care. What if there were a serious accident or an illness that could be blamed on the staff? They knew the church as the program's sponsor would be named in a suit and that it might be hard to defend against allegations of negligence or worse yet, child abuse.

Others worried about complying with city codes and wondered where the church could get the money for the major remodeling that seemed needed. Still others wondered if the success of the program was actually the key issue. Was it claiming too much energy from the pastor and the other church leaders, as well as standing in the way of the emergence of other ministries?

Listening Meetings

From that first brief discussion of the day care question came an unusual next step. Hearing the concerns of the pastor and sensing some of the other concerns from members, someone proposed that the church organize a series of four "listening meetings" during a three-week period. The clerk explained that no decisions would be made at the meetings. The meetings would have but one simple purpose: to listen to one another's concerns and thoughts. Above all, the goal would be to listen to what God was saying about the future of the program. While all would be welcome to attend, attendance was not required.

Week after week people came and participated in the listening meetings. When they later looked back on the entire discernment process, they felt particularly grateful for the listening meetings. One participant said he found it helpful to "listen to other people's hearts, listen to the Spirit, particularly as the Spirit spoke to me about it." One attendee said that of more value than the information she gathered was her deepened awareness of the feelings of both the proponents and opponents of the day care. Before she attended the meetings, she said she had no idea people felt as strongly as they did. Another participant spoke of the very different feelings and perspectives she carried away from each of the listening meetings. Different people attended each meeting thereby producing a varied combination of perspectives, thoughts, concerns, and fears. "These weren't facts that were changing me," she said. "It was people's hearts that were touching mine. You have to be different after you hear people's hearts."

No one spoke of being manipulated in a particular direction during the listening meetings, for no proposals were on the table to support or oppose. But some spoke of feeling uncomfortable with listening to the strong feelings of other members with no mechanism at hand for resolving the differences. One participant, who liked the process, compared it to making soup over a period of days, adding ingredients along the way in the form of new information and insights. He said the end result was far better than a quicker, more concise gathering of thoughts. Another member said he felt led to stay away from the meetings, that he was to obey by allowing the process to go forward and to support it, but not to take part.

One member expressed the positive outcome of the listening meetings in this way: "The meetings were very refreshing for me because there was no expectation of a particular outcome. So people could say what they needed to say. Although we're not judgmental that much anyway, still there was just the matter of getting things out there without having to take immediate action and being able to see people's feelings and thoughts." Other participants in the listening meetings agreed with that summary. By the time the meetings had finished, the group members felt more than ready to move into the decision-making part of the process.

Deciding to Continue the Program

A few days after the last of the listening meetings, the church's presiding clerk called a special business meeting to process the outcome of the gatherings. In doing so, she felt a great deal of concern about what lay ahead.

"I didn't see any way that it could come out all right," she said. "It had the potential of splitting us terribly, terribly, and irrevocably. There was sheer panic inside of me. The only thing that held me was that I knew that God was God and that God could do something I couldn't see."

God was indeed present in that first decision process, according to the recollections of the members. The meeting began with a summary of the listening meetings. Agreement followed that the church should continue the day care ministry. Clearly the church had work to do and this work needed to be delegated to several committees. One would start the search for a new director; one would work on organizational changes. Another would concentrate on financial matters; still another would devote itself to praying for the working groups. Contrary to the clerk's expectations, this stage of the process went forward smoothly.

Some members sensed that while the decision felt acceptable at the time, they would need to continue working with it in the days ahead. One member recalled, "I had the feeling that it wasn't right, but I was willing to accept it anyway, not knowing for sure if that was just my own bias or what. I didn't feel clear to speak up and say, 'This isn't right.' So I basically just went with the recommendation of the people who had been involved in the process. I trusted the process and I trusted the people to be listening to the Holy Spirit."

Another participant expressed disappointment that some members had taken part in the decision making without having attended the listening meetings. She also felt disappointed that some who had spoken helpfully in the listening meetings did not choose to speak in the business meeting. On the other side of the ledger, a member who had been involved with day care work for many years felt delighted with the outcome, believing the day care to be one of the church's most important community services.

Addressing New Issues

Some in the church hoped that they had left the decision to continue the day care program behind them and no further discussion would be necessary. That was not to be.

A serious issue arose between staff and some parents of children attending the day care. This plunged the congregation once again into considering the problematic aspects of the day care ministry. Although the board later resolved the personnel issue, the turmoil around the situation raised a new question. Was this present crisis simply a natural obstacle to be dealt with, or was this an indication that they might not have arrived at a final decision?

Reopening the Issue

While some would have preferred not to resume discussions about the day care program, the subject simply couldn't be avoided. Some had begun to feel a higher level of concern about the safety of the children because of some serious problems with the building.

At a business meeting, some members began to sense the need to return to the decision about continuing to sponsor the day care program. One member in particular kept asking if the new issues before them meant they must reconsider their earlier decision. The clerk was keenly aware of the strong feelings on both sides of the question. Some had no desire to go back to the sponsorship question; others felt the church had no other choice but to do so.

The clerk in this business meeting helped those on both sides understand that they didn't need to make the final decision that night, but that clearly the group had been led to put the question back on the table. That led to the conclusion that reopening the discussion required more information. Shortly thereafter, the church hired a consultant to do a facilities and program evaluation. This would include information about insurance coverage, finances, adequacy of staff and volunteers, necessary upgrades in the facilities, and how to give the curriculum a stronger denominational emphasis.

At the next business meeting, the consultant gave her report. It became clear from the complexity of the issues that a smaller group needed to study the recommendations and develop a plan. The members agreed to appoint a working group, made up of the pastor, the clerk of the business meeting, the clerk of the elders, and the day care committee. They were to consider the options of maintaining the status quo, operating a preschool only, or ceasing to sponsor day care entirely.

Reversing the Initial Decision

As the clearness committee met, its members began to discern that the program could not continue as it was. In fact, it could not continue without a great deal of work and a new congregational commitment.

As a key member of that working group, the pastor felt a growing conviction that she must express her increasing discomfort with these new challenges. She spoke about her initial call to come to the church and affirmed that she had a clear calling to pastoral work and that this hadn't changed. It also seemed clear that she would not be able to exercise the full range of her gifts as pastor if she continued to be preoccupied with the day care issues. So when the working group met, she expressed this new understanding about how the day care program negatively affected her ministry. The pastor found it hard to speak her thoughts, but that prompted among the others at the meeting a greater degree of openness about the misgivings they also felt.

One individual at the working meeting described a significant shift in her own thinking as a result of the pastor's remarks. This member had been involved with the day care program for a long time and had still considered it an important ministry. When she realized that the program was hindering the pastor's ministry, she became more willing to accept the need for some rethinking. At the end of the meeting, each member expressed how he or she felt. A number said they simply felt tired. They recognized the limited energies of the people in the congregation and also knew that God might be leading them toward some new ministries. They realized they didn't have the energy for the financial and organizational challenges involved in continuing the day care program.

As a group, they sensed that God was most likely saying it was time to let go of the day care ministry. They agreed they should not move in that direction out of fear or out of frustration, but should do so only if they felt sure they were receiving a clear leading from God.

At a pivotal moment during the meeting, one longtime member said God brought a verse to her attention indicating it would be sinful to fail to do what the group knew God would have it do. She took this to mean that the many shortcomings of the building were not just aesthetic questions, for they were putting at risk the safety of the children and the leaders. To become aware of these problems and look the other way would be disobedience.

Thus was birthed a new insight within the working group that it should take a recommendation to the next business meeting to end the church's sponsorship of the day care. To make sure this did not catch anyone off guard, the committee members notified all church members that they were going to bring this recommendation to the business meeting.

After many months—during which this issue occupied almost all the energies of the members—the last steps in the process happened quickly. Those who had invested years in nurturing the program had nearly reached the point of feeling ready to release it. One member said she felt that the church had been right all along that day care was a valuable ministry and the children deserved a high quality program. But in the business meeting she came to understand that the church was no longer called to operate the day care—that God would provide another sponsoring agency and another building. This insight lifted a heavy burden from her and from some others in the meeting.

Even though the sentiments of most members shifted quickly in the direction of severing ties with the day care program, many people expressed feelings of sadness and loss. Tears flowed and members ministered to one another's grief. In time, the sadness gave way to a feeling of settledness about the way forward that had come during the hard times.

In looking back at that final decision and the entire seven-month process, one person said she felt that what made the process work was the obedience of every person to God's voice.

She declared, "It brings tears to my eyes, how precious every single person was, because there was a true sense that no matter what the pain, or what the cost, or whether it went against us or for us, every person was trying to listen and be faithful to that as best they knew how. It's a tender thing in the life of the meeting to know that we can face tough stuff and we'll all be faithful. Yes, it may take time. And yes, we may not come to the perfect answer the first time out. But we have the capability of hearing God and doing it. Boy, that's wonderful."

4

THE INDIVIDUAL ENTERS INTO THE DECISION-MAKING PROCESS

Lon Fendall

As we saw in the Seattle case study, individuals have a crucial role to play in prayerful listening as part of the group's discernment and decision making. The Holy Spirit may direct that the individual help with the group's process by speaking to the issue. How and when should the individual speak?

Speaking as Part of Discernment

Scripture cautions us many times to refrain from speaking in certain situations. In the King James Version of the Bible, this concept is commonly expressed "hold your peace."

The book of James warns us about the great evil that can come from speaking inappropriately: "The tongue also is a fire, a world of evil among the parts of the body. It corrupts the whole person, sets the whole course of his life on fire, and is itself set on fire by hell" (James 3:6). That might suggest that we take a vow of silence, like members of some monastic orders. But the opposite conclusion can be drawn from another passage of Scripture:

> A word aptly spoken is like apples of gold in settings of silver. Like an earring of gold or an ornament of fine gold is a wise man's rebuke to a listening ear. Like the coolness of snow at harvest time is a trustworthy messenger

to those who send him; he refreshes the spirit of his masters. (Proverbs 25:11-13)

In the context of the group discernment process, how do we know when we are to speak? The short answer is that we must speak when and only when God tells us to speak. We are to speak when we can't help doing so, when we would be disobeying our Lord to keep our mouths shut. This may mean speaking much less frequently than we are accustomed to doing. Thomas Kelly talks about the awesome experience of being used by God to express God's truth to other believers:

> We seem to be acted upon by a More-than-ourselves, who stills our time-torn spirits and breathes into us, as on Creation's day, the breath of life. When one rises to speak in such a meeting one has a sense of *being used*, of being played upon, of being spoken through.[1]

Kelly's view of being used by God to convey truth and leading is a high standard to achieve. Much of the time we fall short of this ideal. But it should be our guide in determining when to speak, what tone to adopt, and what content to include. The imperfections of our speaking haunt us, limitations that the prophet Isaiah called "unclean lips." But God responded to Isaiah's feeling of inadequacy by having an angel come to him and touch his lips with a live coal as a symbol of being delivered from wrong speaking and the feeling of inadequacy (see Isaiah 6).

Consider a few guidelines for speaking in a way that moves the discernment process forward:

Recognition—An important part of hearing God's voice is to allow the clerk to guide the discussion and to allow time between the statements for reflecting and processing. After a reasonable amount of time has passed, one should ask the leader to be recognized instead of beginning to speak as soon as others stop speaking. People engaging in conversations often interrupt one another, but this should not be the pattern in discernment meetings.

Respect—We help the group discernment process by always speaking respectfully about our fellow believers. We resist the temptation to slip in negative comments about others in the group. This is difficult, for one form of discernment is evaluating the work of a staff member or a volunteer involved in the group's ministry. Is it possible to talk about someone's unsatisfactory performance, while remaining respectful toward that person? Yes, it's possible—but not easy! The Bible contains a host of "judge not" commands, based on the sense that each of us is created by God and is worthy of respect. We are to be very careful about demeaning others' work or personhood.

Brevity—Nothing frustrates more than to leave a meeting for discernment, realizing that the business could have been concluded in half the time if the participants had stated their points without repetition and irrelevant additions. It's very hard for a clerk to interrupt people to ask them to shorten their comments. So the best means of controlling the length of speaking is self-discipline. If we ourselves say only what is helpful and what is aimed toward discerning God's leading, we can hope that others will follow our example. I was in a discernment meeting that went on for a long time, partly because people kept repeating the thoughts and ideas of others who had already spoken. When others say what we have been thinking, we can rejoice that we have been led similarly—but there is no need to repeat their comments. In this situation we might simply say, "Others have already expressed my thinking and I'm in full support of the action being proposed."

Clarity—We've all probably heard people say they were "thinking out loud" and that they did not yet feel certain about their conclusions. In some ways, this can be healthy in a discernment meeting. Expressing leadings and nudgings still not fully formed can begin to move the group toward greater clarity. Discernment is a work in process and it is good to express our thoughts as we understand them at the time. But we should avoid muddled speaking and verbal wanderings.

Clarity is not the same as finality. We don't help the process of discernment by locking into our first impressions and thoughts. God may have a great deal more to say on the subject, so we have to remain ready to hear God's voice during the discernment process. We should pray to see things clearly. We can identify with the words of Paul about seeing a poor reflection in a mirror (or as the King James Version has it, seeing "through a glass, darkly," 1 Corinthians 13:12). But we should clean off our spiritual mirrors and eyeglasses to be able to think clearly and to express ourselves as clearly as possible.

Releasing Our Words and Leadings to Focus on God's Leading

The discernment process calls us to present our words and thoughts with no strings attached. We are not to cling to those insights as though they were fully formed and not subject to discussion.

Perhaps we've known people who have such a fragile self-identity that they can't deal with questions about their statements. They take any criticism as a negative judgment. That must not be our posture as we offer our words and ideas in the discernment process.

Occasionally the apostle Paul exaggerated about his own feelings of unworthiness, even saying at times that he felt worthless. He wasn't struggling with an underdeveloped sense of self-worth, however; he was trying to show us by example that we should not become too impressed with our own accomplishments and insights. We should not get too attached to the ideas we bring into the discernment process. In Romans 12, Paul takes a balanced approach to the individual's contribution to the group process. In *The Message*, Paul's teaching sounds like this:

> So here's what I want you to do, God helping you: Take your everyday, ordinary life—your sleeping, eating, going-to-work, and walking-around life—and place it before God as an offering. Embracing what God does for you is the best thing you can do for him....Readily recognize what he wants from you, and quickly respond to it. Unlike the culture around you, always dragging you down to its level of immaturity, God brings the best out of you, develops well-formed maturity in you....Living then, as every one of you does, in pure grace, it's important that you not misinterpret yourselves as people who are bringing this goodness to God. No, God brings it all to you. The only accurate way to understand ourselves is by what God is and by what he does for us, not by what we are and what we do for him....So since we find ourselves fashioned into all these excellently formed and marvelously functioning parts in Christ's body, let's just go ahead and be what we were made to be, without enviously or pridefully comparing ourselves with each other, or trying to be something we aren't." (Romans 12:1-6a)

The Old Testament practice of presenting animals and produce as offerings and sacrifices feels very different from our contemporary styles of worship. But maybe we can picture ourselves presenting verbal and conceptual offerings instead of lambs or grain. We freely bring our words and ideas to the group in obedience to God's prompting. We do not know or care how the offerings might be used in God's service, for we have given them away. If our ideas should happen to become a central part of the group's discernment, we can be thankful but not boastful. If they fade into the background, we are equally thankful, for that which replaces them has taken on more enduring power and usefulness. If they turn out to be wrong or not useful, there is no shame for putting them on the table for consideration. Sometimes God even uses a wrong idea to move the group to a new way of conceptualizing the way forward.

In the Romans 12 passage, Paul warns believers not to enviously or pridefully compare themselves with others. The tempter wants us to slip in a reference to *my* proposal, *my* recommendation, *my* solution, instead of using the more appropriate plural pronoun, *our.* Nothing of enduring value that comes from group discernment is the result of an individual person's contribution. The individual thoughts have blended into the whole and are no longer recognizable, like the flour, eggs, and sugar that become a plateful of brownies.

An even more compelling reason to guard against pride of authorship in group discernment is that anything of ultimate value comes from God, not from us. In the passage in Romans 12, the apostle reminds us that "the only accurate way to understand ourselves is by what God is and by what he does for us, not by what we are and what we do for him." The person clerking the group discernment process should not have to worry about our being offended if the group is led away from the thoughts we have presented. We do not hang on to "our" offering, but we rejoice that the group is moving ever closer to God's way forward.

Being Good Stewards of Our Influence

People in many cultures feel and express great respect for the elderly, the wise, and those in leadership. The more typical pillars of American culture, on the other hand, laud the notions of equal worth and individual attainment. Our culture gives too little deference to people of advanced years, of greater seniority in the group, and people whose insights in the past have helped reach clarity in group decisions.

Nevertheless, Americans have a certain amount of respect toward people who seem to have greater insight than others. Some have called this quality "weightiness." The idea is that all are equal, but some may be more equal than others! If it were a voting situation, it would be like giving some people more votes, since they have such good judgment and common sense.

This can actually be a positive consideration in group discernment if the undergirding principle of bringing *every* offering to the discernment of the group is observed. The person of considerable influence is called to be a good steward of his or her reputation for being a reliable conduit of God's messages. If he or she has not received a compelling message from God at a given time, he or she should not speak. God will speak through others at that time. The person's position or reputation does not call for him or her to be a part of every discussion. The book of Proverbs expresses the virtue of self-restraint in a humorous way: "Even dunces who keep quiet are thought to be wise; as long as they keep their mouths shut, they're smart" (17:28 *The Message*).

Nevertheless, in a discernment meeting we should be ready to hear God speak through those whom we know to be wise and discerning individuals. They may be elderly or young, lifelong Christians or newer followers. They may be pastors or elders, called of God to those positions because they meet the biblical criteria for spiritual leadership. It is a terrible mistake to make it difficult for leaders in a group to bring their expertise and experience to bear on a particular question. It is also a mistake to expect these leaders to have a word from the Lord on every question. All believers stand on level ground at the foot of the cross. Leaders will feel led to speak on some questions and not on others. Avoid any unwritten rule that the group cannot move forward until it has heard from certain "weighty" members.

Pride is a great sin and the respected leader, the "weighty" person, might be tempted to let the discussion go ahead without speaking, even when he or she could help the discussion move forward with timely thoughts. Then, when everyone seems to have spoken except him or her, the person "weighs in," making it very difficult to reach closure because that person waited so long to contribute to the process. This strategy is a perverse way of reminding everyone of the person's clout— that no decisions can be made without taking into account his or her views. The influential person must learn to speak on a timely basis or not at all.

Recognizing and Assenting to the Holy Spirit's Leading

A person doesn't need to be the leader to recognize that God is actively guiding the group. The clerk has much of the responsibility in bringing people along in the discernment process toward closure, but should not be expected to shape that process entirely by himself or herself. A sense of joy often erupts when a participant sees and names the movement of God in helping the group advance; and then the clerk can help the group proceed with what that faithfulness entails.

The apostle Paul urged believers in Ephesus to cooperate with God in helping them become skillful in discernment:

> I ask—ask the God of our Master, Jesus Christ, the God of glory—to make you intelligent and discerning in knowing him personally, your eyes focused and clear, so that you can see exactly what it is he is calling you to do, grasp the immensity of this glorious way of life he has for his followers, oh, the utter extravagance of his work in us who trust him—endless energy, boundless strength! (Ephesians 1:17-19 *The Message*)

This text points to the ways individuals can discern what God seems to be saying in a particular situation:

- We need to use the intelligence God has given us.
- The better we know Christ, the more we will be able to discern Christ's leading.
- We should keep our spiritual eyes clear and focused.
- We should expect that God's ways of moving forward will be much more exciting than anything we might design.

We will often be called to discern God's voice in what others are saying. Once again, Acts 15 provides an excellent example of this. James listened carefully to the defenders of the status quo—the Pharisees—but also to Peter, Paul, and Barnabas. Even as one of the Jerusalem believers who had been skeptical about downplaying Jewish traditions, James heard God's voice in what was being said in the meeting.

James said essentially that the comments he heard in the meeting drew him to a passage from the prophet Amos, who spoke of the Gentiles bearing God's name. He said it had become clear to him that God was leading the council to lighten the burden on the new Gentile believers. God was asking them to do only a few things, such as being sexually pure and not eating food offered to idols. The members of the council immediately knew that James was expressing God's leading. They had no further need for discussion (Acts 15:13-21).

As we noted earlier, the letter from the Jerusalem council to the believers in Antioch contains a marvelous phrase that captures the ideal of people acting in agreement with God's direction: "It seemed good to the Holy Spirit and to us." The group had come to this powerful oneness with God's direction because of careful listening to others and to God—even though the group consisted of a large number of individuals and groups who had come into the meeting in support of opposite outcomes. Nevertheless, people on both sides of the question heard God guiding them individually toward a new position.

Those who came to the Jerusalem meeting hoping to remove all restrictions on the Gentile Christians had to understand that they were not "getting their way." It was God's way. And it required that those defending the position of the Antioch Christians had to develop a much more gracious view of their opponents in Jerusalem. One side didn't move to the other side. In this situation, both sides moved to the middle, where the Holy Spirit invited them to embrace a future in which spiritual transformation, not legalism, would be the defining characteristic of the movement.

A PASTOR ACCEPTS A CALL
TO ANOTHER CHURCH

This case study shows the ways an individual's decision can impact a Christian group. A pastor received a call from another church and realized that his current church would benefit from being included in the discernment process. In doing so, everyone learned important lessons about listening to God and remaining attentive to the need for people to know what is happening—and that God loves the church much more than any of us imagine.

Nothing about the situation seemed fair. The pastor had come from a large church to be part of a team to lead a smaller church in Boise, Idaho, through a healing process after a traumatic split. Later he was asked to consider returning to the church from which he had come.

Some in Boise assumed such a thing might happen eventually, but couldn't believe God would take their beloved pastoral couple after they had been at the church for only a few years. It seemed to some that their situation was a little like Nathan's story to King David, about a rich man with many sheep and cattle and a poor man with one lamb (see 2 Samuel 12). In the story, the rich man needed some meat to serve a visitor. He spared his own herds of livestock and took the poor man's only lamb for the meal.

Church splits leave deep scars, and this church in Boise had plenty of scars. But thanks to some excellent steps in individual and group discernment, and thanks to God's faithfulness in speaking to people ready to listen, the pastor's leaving did not result in a new experience of trauma. Over a period of time, nearly everyone in the church came to understand that it was God who was calling one of their pastors to return to his former church. It didn't thrill the people to lose a fine pastor, but eventually they felt able to release this faithful and much-loved couple. The pastors and the people learned a great deal about following God's leading through the process.

This experience illustrates a type of discernment quite different from the Acts 15 type of decision making. The church held a number of meetings in which discernment was the focal point, but the church would not make this decision. The choice facing the church lay in another direction: whether they would release their pastor to follow God's leading and in so doing to learn more about listening to God.

The Pastor Struggles with Whether to Consider Leaving

The first few weeks of the process did not involve most people in the church, for the pastor did not yet feel it was appropriate to speak about the contact he had received from folks at the former church. Only the copastors at the Boise church knew about this. The copastors had come as part of the pastoral team whose principal challenge had been rebuilding the church after the major split. The pastoral couples had known each other before going to Boise and continued to be close friends and effective coworkers during their ministry.

One couple recalled how difficult it felt to be talking regularly with the other couple about whether they would apply for the job at their former church. This kind of information had to be kept confidential, so the copastors could talk only to each other and to God during that time.

During these talks, the couple who had been asked to move expressed their ambivalence about applying for the position. Some days they felt this might be something God was directing them to do; on other days they felt sure it was not the right time to consider the move. They felt they needed a few more years of experience before taking on the leadership of a large church. They talked to some friends and spiritual advisors outside the church, but didn't receive any definite insights from those discussions. Some thought they should pursue it, but others did not feel sure.

The Elders Meeting

At the beginning of a regular meeting of the elders, the pastor said he had something to tell the group and would do so at the end of the meeting. Only the copastor knew what that meant. That copastor sat through the meeting, not able to concentrate on the business because of the pain of knowing the step his teammates were considering could mean the end of a wonderful partnership in ministry.

The pastor's announcement at the end of the meeting caught everyone but the copastor off guard. No one knew what to say. During the inevitable post-meeting conversations, a number in the group thought they weren't likely to lose their pastor, for they believed God would never take him away when he was needed so much in Boise. "God wouldn't do that to us," one of the elders remembered saying.

Some felt upset that the search committee at the other church hadn't talked to the elders of the Boise church before inviting the pastor to apply. The elders were a long way from feeling they could let their pastor go with their blessing. They discerned at that time that God wasn't through with the pastors in Boise.

The Entire Church Joins the Discernment Process

One thing that helped in the later stages of the process was that the pastor acted quickly to inform the entire church what was happening. Soon after his announcement in the elders meeting, the other church invited him to visit for an interview, and he felt clear about accepting the invitation. After he had done this, he sent a letter to his church members telling them what he had done. He said he was trusting that God would close or open doors to his ministry in this other church in a way that would be good for both churches and for everyone involved. But for those who had hoped he wouldn't become a finalist, it became clear that the process was moving in that direction.

In a letter, the pastor invited church members to a meeting for prayer and discussion about the decision he and his wife were facing and the impact it might have on the church. At the meeting the pastor talked about his contacts with the other church, about how he and his wife were feeling about the process to that point, and then invited people to ask questions. He explained what it meant to be "called" to a position, saying that it was a combination of the leaders in the other church discerning who should be called and the recognition on the part of everyone that the ultimate call must come from God.

The pastor announced in this general meeting that he and his wife were sensing that they needed another church meeting to focus more intensely on the "clearness" process. He said he had in mind some people he hoped would participate, who were experienced in listening to God. But he also said he wanted others to feel welcome at the meeting. He asked, though, that those who planned to attend first study some material on spiritual discernment he would make available.

Before the meeting for clearness, the copastors called another general meeting to help church members process their feelings of impending loss. They had been reading about a family that used the "prayer of *examen*" (see the glossary for a further explanation of this form of prayer). When the wife and mother of the family found out she had terminal cancer, the prayer helped the family deal with their grief. It focused their praying around the "desolations" they felt and the "consolations" they claimed on the positive side.

For some, the situation in the church paralleled what would be experienced by a grieving family. The church might lose its pastor so the grieving process had already begun, even though the event had not occurred. Would that grieving lead the people into the arms of God or downward into their own despair? That was the question. Together, the gathering worked through the prayer of examen, a familiar process to many in the church.

As the process went forward, people individually listened to God and wrote down the feelings of desolation and consolation that came to them in the quietness. One of the participants recalled that providing this structure for the prayer time helped a great deal. She and others who had survived the traumatic split the church had previously experienced had great fear that the negative aspects of that time would repeat themselves. But the time of listening to God and sharing the results helped that group express their fear and anger and balance these emotions with the certainties of God's love for the church and constancy during a time of change.

After the points of desolation and consolation were discussed and listed for all to see, there came a time to reflect on these realities. Someone noticed that the consolations were all based on things they could be sure about, like the unchanging love of God and God's compassion for the church. The desolations, on the other hand, were based on things that might or might not happen. The pastor *might* leave. It *might* be difficult to find another pastor. The copastor *might* experience heavy burdens in the pastoral work during the transition time. Some people who had unpleasant memories from the previous church split *might* not want to experience new uncertainties and *might* leave the church—fear-based, every one of them.

Looking at the lists in this way helped people see that the *mights* would probably not all come about and that there was a greater *might* that they could draw on, namely, the infinite strength of God. They also affirmed that they did not want to be motivated by fear.

Participants in this meeting later recalled some of the other positive aspects of the process:

- They learned they didn't need to assume there would be another breakdown in community like the one that happened during the split.

- Expressing fears and anger helped others to name and process their own feelings.

- Everyone was being valued enough to be invited into the process, even though it wasn't clear at the time how their collective expressions would be handled.

- For each person to be asked to share what God was saying to him or her, meant they each had to be sure they were listening to God and not just speaking from their own thoughts and biases. That required a strong prayer life.

Another benefit of both of these general meetings was the increased confidence and trust the pastors felt in including the people of the church in their discernment steps. Even though they had announced in the first meeting that there would be a later meeting for clearness, they still felt concerned about the potential negative impact of including others in the process. But the people in the general meetings had been able to express their emotions in a constructive way. They had come to understand that their task was not to argue with the pastor about leaving, but to listen to God to see if it might indeed be God's plan for the pastor to go to another church. From those insights, the pastors concluded it would be a good thing, not a harmful thing, to continue to include the church in the discernment process.

The Meeting for Clearness

Between the time of the general meetings and the meeting for clearness, the other church extended the call to the pastor to be their senior pastor. Since the call now changed from a possibility to a reality, the meeting for clearness became very important—and potentially difficult.

The fact that the pastor and his wife had welcomed the people of the church into their discernment process meant that the meeting mattered greatly. The central question was what the pastor would do about the invitation to lead the other church. Because of the importance of the meeting, they invited a person outside the church to come and clerk the meeting—someone people in the church knew and trusted, someone highly regarded in the denomination and with no particular tie to either of the churches involved.

One participant in the clearness meeting recalls looking around the room as the meeting started and feeling surprised by the size of the group and who was there. It had been made clear that the purpose of the meeting was not to make a decision nor to take the discernment process out of the couple's hands. People were there to listen to God and to share what God had been saying to them since the process started. The pastors and the participants felt pleased that 20 people were willing to be part of such a meeting.

In keeping with the purpose of the meeting, no one kept minutes and no decision was crafted at the end. People shared openly and helpfully about what God was saying to them. Several insights came from the meeting, including:

- God had been doing some very significant healing in the church, as evidenced by the way people were dealing with the issue. They had reached a much deeper level of communication with God.

- No matter how clear people might become that God had called the pastor and his wife to return to the other church, their going would create a deep feeling of loss.

- People could either choose to hang on to that loss or step forward into God's power to carry the church forward.

- Dealing with these questions would help people deal with the fact that other prayers might not be answered as they hoped.

Without it ever being said at the end of the meeting, it became clear to the pastors and to the other participants that their pastor was being released to accept the call to the other church. But it also became clear that it would be a challenge to extend that leading from the clearness group to the rest of the congregation. Some people had apparently made a point of not attending the meetings, for they did not yet feel ready to accept the possibility that the changes ahead could be part of God's plan. There would be no church business meeting to decide about releasing the pastor. And even if there were, it wouldn't matter, in the opinion of these folks. The pastor would leave anyway.

Immediately after the meeting for clearness, the pastor sent church members an e-mail reporting on the meeting and the release he and his wife felt to go back to the other church. In the e-mail he said:

> My prayer for months has been that God would clearly lead us to stay in Boise or to go to another church. Way back in December, I sensed clearly from God that if we were to leave Boise, three things would have to happen: the other church would have to be unified in that call to us; we would need to receive a personal sense of leading that way; and that somehow there would be a release from the church in Boise. As of tonight, all three of those things have happened in clearer ways than I would have dared hope. I'm overwhelmed by God's care, and love, and graciousness in giving wisdom when we ask.

In the same e-mail, the pastor also described those who attended the meeting and the spirit of love that characterized it:

> I was overwhelmed by the love they expressed to us, and their willingness to enter this process and seek God with us when they knew it could mean personal loss to them. They did it, and they grieve us leaving, but they feel peace. Sitting here after almost six months of wrestling and questioning, there is no answer for that to me other than God at work.

He concluded his message to the people with an appeal for them to unite around the church's needs in the days ahead:

> Now we enter a new phase here, and one where a lot of prayer is still needed. I'd like to ask that you pray for the

co-pastors in this transition and new phase of ministry. Pray for the many people who weren't a part of this meeting here and are still having a very difficult time accepting it. Pray for hope to prevail over despair in our church community as a whole. And pray that the right person will be led here and one who can serve this community and be a good partner with the co-pastors in every sense of the word.

Solidifying the Clearness Process

The release the couple felt in the clearness meeting lifted the burden of uncertainty about what they were to do and whether the church could support them in going to a new ministry. But when they went to the new community to consult with the church and to look for a house, feelings of sadness and loss engulfed the worship service in Boise.

Those who hadn't chosen to take part in the discernment meetings felt upset, but were unwilling to express their feelings. At one point in the service the copastor said, "There's an elephant in the room and nobody's talking about it, but everybody's thinking about it." He invited people to address the issue directly in the open worship time—and they did. Some of those who hadn't been at the meetings expressed some of the same feelings of loss and sadness that had come out in those meetings. One of the elders responded to those expressions by noting it was not always a comfortable and happy thing to follow God, but they could trust a loving God to act in a way that would help—not hurt—their church.

The elders concluded after that worship service that they needed to provide a concrete way for people to express their trust in God and their conviction that the pastoral couple would not have agreed to leave if God had not called them. So with the help of the pastor, the elders prepared a "minute" addressed to the other church—a way to address the ill will some people still felt toward the other church for "stealing" their beloved pastor. It was short, honest, and loving:

> We want to commission our pastors and their family to the loving care of your church. Even though we are saddened at their leaving, we believe that this is God's will for them as well as for us and for you. This decision has come with much prayer, listening and trying to discern the voice and heart of God. We commend them to your care with all our love and support. We ask that you treat them with kindness and Godly love. We trust that they will experience your full support and encouragement and share in your joys and sorrows as they walk alongside you in ministry.

People in the Boise church were invited to sign the minute. Many did, and this opportunity provided a way for them to process their grieving. Some chose not to sign the minute and they felt no pressure to do so. But those who did sign felt it was a better thing to do than pouting over the idea of a large church taking a valued pastor from a smaller church.

People in the other church felt deeply grateful to receive the minute from the Boise church and wrote their own minute in response. It too was short and filled with love and gratitude for the spirit of the Boise minute:

> We are grateful for the unity we have with you in Christ. We recognize that your process of releasing your pastors and their family into our care was not done easily, and involved much prayer and listening to God. Thank you for the love you have showered on them and on us. We are humbled by the grace and love you have demonstrated during this time of transition. We accept your charge for us to love and support this family as they walk

alongside us in ministry. We feel a special bond with you, and are committed to continue praying for you as you serve the Boise area with the love and light of Christ. Praise be to God for His great love, and may He richly bless you.

Participants in the business meeting that approved this minute asked their clerk to deliver the minute in person to Boise, something like the step taken at the end of the discernment process recorded in Acts 15. One leader at the Boise church remembers her feelings on hearing the minute from the other church: "It was almost like, 'The End' to a good story. When you do this right, this way, it's a good thing. It doesn't feel like something's been ripped away from you, but more that it's just another step and you keep on moving."

Laying a Foundation for Future Discernment

If the discernment process around the departure of the pastoral couple had resulted in a great deal of bitterness, people leaving, and even a new split in the church, the process of calling a new pastoral couple would have been a struggle as well. As it was, the many things learned about listening to God and interacting with other believers about God's direction carried over into the selection of a new pastor.

People did not feel terribly alarmed when differences of opinion arose regarding some of the candidates. They had found ways to express their feelings and turn the focus from these feelings to what God was saying to them. Some who had not been thought of as spiritual anchors in the church now found their place as strong discerners of God's leading. And the new pastors were able to step right into the flow of those ready to move into new places of spiritual growth and outreach.

The discernment process continued through the calling of an associate pastor. The prayer of examen was again used in a search committee meeting. Sunday morning worship service became the final business meeting to consider and approve the candidate. The entire congregation had another opportunity to participate in the practice of personal and corporate discernment. It had become part of the church's story and ongoing life.

5

THE LEADER'S ROLE IN GROUP DISCERNMENT

Jan Wood

The leader of the group discernment process has a different function than a chairperson, president, or moderator.* We prefer to use the term *clerk* for the leader of group discernment.

Clerking is a distinct form of leadership. It is the practical way to implement and fully acknowledge that God is an active presence and partner in all the activities of life (see Ephesians 1:19-22). It takes into account that no one person knows the mind and heart of God fully. The wonder of God's plan is that God distributes a wide assortment of expertise among people (see Romans 12; Ephesians 4; 1 Corinthians 12), making visible the invisible movement of God's Spirit in the group.

While clerking is empowering in many settings and organizations, it is especially appropriate in the church and in organizations trying to be faithful to the lordship of Christ. This is one form that matches function.

Understanding How God Works in Groups

The first step in learning how to perform effectively as a clerk is to take a step back from the details and duties of the job to get clear about how God works among us.

---

* *Even though the process of clerking is different from being a president, chairperson, or moderator, it is completely possible to lead through group discernment in organizations that use these titles.*

1. God can work with any group. Your group probably has varied expertise, maturity, and experiences. The group probably will include people of many theological perspectives and convictions. A typical group will have strong and forceful personalities who know a lot about how things should be done. It will have quiet individuals inclined to withhold their thoughts and discernments, but who have excellent ideas. Most groups will have a troublesome person or two.

There is no such thing as a perfect group. We all become part of the miracle of being God's people just as we are. Everyone and every group is a mix of glory and brokenness—and that's why any group that gathers to be faithful to God's motions must begin with simple humility. It is just as unlikely that anything coherent could come from the likes of us as it was that the motley assortment of men from Galilee could change the course of history. Yet in the full reality of what God is working with, we gather to experience miracles of the Holy Spirit. The loaves and fish of our group *are* enough to feed the multitudes!

God doesn't need a different group of people. God is fully capable of working through this group, exactly as it is. The clerk, first and foremost, embodies this conviction even when others lose sight of it. God can—and is—working in and through this gathered group of people. The clerk has faith in God and in the group when its members can't see their way forward.

2. The miracle of Pentecost is that God dwells in our midst. God doesn't sit aloof in the sky, trusting that God's followers will somehow get it right. God doesn't reserve attention for the big decisions. God fully partners with us in the totality of this adventure of life.

In the New Testament, the Holy Spirit was as interested in the fairness of seating arrangements (Acts 6:1-3) as in saving Paul's life (Acts 27). The God who created the earth with such precision can certainly lead a group to get a city permit on time! The same God who attends to the flight path of a butterfly has a heart for the yearnings of God's precious people. The same God who is all-wise is smart about financial matters. The God who transformed a Saul of Tarsus can deal with the likes of you and me—and "them." The clerk carries this unflagging knowledge of God through thick and thin.

3. Giftedness is distributed among people like interlocking pieces of a puzzle. God could have given all the expertise to a few anointed leaders and let it go at that. But God had a more exquisite plan. Each person carries a part of the puzzle; no one carries it all. A Paul needed a Priscilla or a Barnabas or a Silas, and vice versa. No one in the body of Christ operates alone, even if he or she appears to be serving alone. For example, the person gifted in serving others must have structures created by the person who has the gift of administration. They all need the focus that comes from the gift of leadership; the boundaries that come from the gift of wisdom; and the empowerment that comes from the gifts of prayer, healing, intercession, and miracles.

The clerk is the symphonic conductor of a group with many gifts. Every group preparing to make a decision has a musical composition in the making. No one really knows the tune until each part gets offered up in its rightful place. There will be no music if the drummer insists on drowning out the oboist. The rests are as important as the notes to be played. The holding back is as important as soaring into a solo. The Holy Spirit calls forth the tune; the clerk facilitates that process.

Sometimes God allows the clerk to hear and know the song. More often the clerk moves the group along with the assurance that the melody will emerge as each person remains faithful to the process.

4. Respect is a mark of Jesus' rule and reign. The instructions to the early church are filled with reminders to respect one another. It is intrinsic to the gospel that we who love God respect all those whom God loves. We respect those who do not yet know God, so that they will sense the authentic love of God through us. We respect others as greater than us. We respect and take extra care of those who seem weak in their faith. We speak respectfully in ways that help, uplift, and edify. Or in the words of Paul,

> ...You're done with that old life. It's like a filthy set of ill-fitting clothes you've stripped off and put in the fire. Now you're dressed in a new wardrobe. Every item of your new way of life is custom-made by the Creator, with his label on it. All the old fashions are now obsolete. Words like Jewish and non-Jewish, religious and irreligious, insider and outsider, uncivilized and uncouth, slave and free, mean nothing. From now on everyone is defined by Christ, everyone is included in Christ.

> So, chosen by God for this new life of love, dress in the wardrobe God picked out for you: compassion, kindness, humility, quiet strength, discipline. Be even-tempered, content with second place, quick to forgive an offense. Forgive as quickly and completely as your Master forgave you. And regardless of what else you put on, wear love. It's your basic, all-purpose garment. Never be without it.

> Let the peace of Christ keep you in tune with each other, in step with each other. None of this going off and doing

your own thing. And cultivate thankfulness. (Colossians 3:9-15 *The Message*)

5. We are an empowered people. Immediately after Pentecost, words became empowered and ordinary men became unshakably courageous (see Acts 2). Jesus' followers received power over evil. No longer did the community of faith need to be held hostage to principalities and powers that can sometimes hijack the business of being God's people. Run-of-the-mill human orneriness can be overcome by an unrelenting commitment to love, forgiveness, and grace for everyone. Unholy spirits—both small and large—can be exiled through words, rather than violence. We meet persecution with the endless love of Christ. We defeat principalities and powers through steadfast faithfulness to the right-side-up ways of Jesus.

Qualifications for Clerking

A clerk must be experienced and comfortable with the process of knowing and trusting God's faithfulness—that's the most important qualification. This process of group discernment assumes that God is present and can be known. It assumes that God can change and transform minds and hearts. It assumes that God is at work even when things look bleak. Trusting God in each moment provides the anchor for making decisions through group discernment.

No single profile of spiritual giftedness exists for effective clerking. The variety of styles of successful clerking reflects the clerk's giftedness, disposition, and maturity. A clerk with a keen sense of discernment is well equipped to sort sense from nonsense. A clerk with the gift of wisdom may often see the integrating ideas that help guide the way forward. Clerks with gifts of leadership or prophecy may do their task assertively, while those with gifts of exhortation or service may appear to accomplish the same thing with a lighter touch.

Clerks serve best if they have a disposition that feels comfortable with ambiguity and process. It will help greatly if they can avoid feeling they have to fix or save situations. They must have the capacity to deal with dissent without getting emotionally caught up in it.

An Overview of Clerking

If you were presiding over a meeting that used a system of voting, you would know the process. It goes something like this: The relevant information is presented to the group. A discussion follows, with people debating the various proposals/possibilities. In due time, there is a motion and a second; and then a vote is taken. A decision is made.

When you are a clerk presiding over a meeting that seeks God's guidance, several simple but different principles apply:

- The group aligns with God's Spirit.

  Key Goal: To be one with God's heart/perspective/Spirit

- Information is presented to the group.

  Key Goal: To empower the group to discern well

- The group waits in listening silence to perceive what God's Spirit is communicating.

  Key Goal: To seek God's wisdom collaboratively

- Group members work together to see how these perceptions fit together.

  Key Goal: To be in the mystery and let God unfold the group knowing

- When the group has a common sense of "yes-ness," the clerk articulates this understanding.

   Key Goal: To accept God's leading for this decision and prepare to be faithful and obedient

- The decision is written into a minute.

   Key Goal: To articulate the truth of what the group has done and is deciding

- The minute is read to the group to double-check that it has captured both the spirit and the facts of the decision.

   Key Goal: To verify this understanding

- Each participant honors the decision as a leading from God.

   Key Goal: To honor Christ who has led this group in this step

Skills of Clerking

To implement these principles, the clerk needs to understand the process and the skills that accompany these steps. The clerk is responsible to structure the listening process for success. Perhaps an easy way to look at the practical skills of clerking is to examine what needs to be done before a meeting, during the meeting, and after the meeting.

Before the Meeting

Prepare Yourself Spiritually. The clerk needs to take special care that his or her own spirit is aligned with Christ's. This translates into holding each person in respect, continuously releasing and forgiving everyone who has littered the minds and hearts of group members with hurts and wounds

(Colossians 3:13). It means maintaining the perspective that Jesus is head of the church and Lord over *all* (Colossians 1). It means resting in the certainty that *all* things work together for good to those who love God and are called according to his purposes (Romans 8:28). This may mean going to talk with a person with whom you are out of fellowship (Matthew 5:21-26).

Organize the Information. *Divide the decision-making process into manageable chunks.* The clerk is responsible to know what needs to be brought to the meeting and what does not. This means understanding which issues are to be brought to the meeting as information and which need group discernment. It also means dividing an item into components that may warrant separate thought and discussion.

Once those things become clear, it is time to think through the process from beginning to end. A flow chart for complex issues often helps the process. A flow chart is a step-by-step chart showing what has to be done in what order—and what is needed for each step of the process. Flow charts can be wonderful tools for the group in anticipating the appropriate sequencing of decisions and actions. It is easy to see that one decision must precede another decision, even when we want to get ahead of the process. The charts can identify general categories of actions for a large project, such as a church relocation. Or the chart can be very detailed to make sure everything is prepared for the youth meeting on Thursday night. If creating charts or thinking through details isn't the clerk's "cup of tea," he or she should enlist a person with the gift of administration to help with these preparations.

It is the task of the clerk to identify the component parts of the process and decide in what order they are to be presented for consideration. Let the group know what they are to decide and where that decision fits into the larger pattern of decisions. Be very specific about what needs to be decided or doesn't need to be decided in this venue at this time.

Provide the Group with Information. In order to ask God the right questions and to listen for useful guidance, group members need to have the appropriate information *before* they come to the decision-making meeting. This information may include a brief background paper on the decision. If a committee has been working on the issue, it might help to give a summary of the committee's process and considerations. If there are technical or complex documents, they may need to be mailed or e-mailed to people so that everyone has time to read them carefully. Give some thought to graphs, diagrams, outlines, pictures, and font variations so that readers don't get lost in a sea of words.

Verify that Key Persons Will Be Available. The wise clerk will identify the key players in the upcoming decision. This may be a committee chairperson or the person with the professional expertise or the person who understands the history of the project. Let these key people know about the projected timeline and verify that their schedules will permit them to participate in the meeting. A glitch as simple as scheduling the budget meeting to occur when the treasurer is on vacation can make a significant difference in the effectiveness of the process!

Allow Enough Time for the Group to Make Successful Decisions. The timing issue has two parts. First, be clear about external deadlines and let the group know about them from the beginning of the process.

"The papers need to be into the bank on…."

"The architectural drawings must be approved and then submitted to the city by…."

Then set the date for consideration far enough in advance of the deadline to allow the work to be done without needless time pressure. Be realistic! If the budget is going to be controversial and difficult, start the process a month earlier than usual. If the business at hand involves many decisions that will need to be packed into a brief period of time, plan to meet more frequently for this specific set of tasks. As a wise clerk, make a habit of building a little extra time into any process. Include enough time for waiting, gathering more information, conversing more together.

The second part of timeliness is to allow enough quality time in any given meeting to complete the decisions on the agenda. Be realistic about how much can be "crammed" into a single meeting. Knowing how difficult it can be to get people together, we sometimes rush through things that need more thought. We try to make decisions long after our minds, bodies, and spirits have ceased to be alert.

If the group has more to consider than time permits, ask God for guidance the same way you ask for other leadings. There is more than one way to accomplish tasks! Be alert to economies of group time. On occasion, have someone time various parts of the meeting. Depending upon the situation, you may find time "leakages." Is everything set up and ready to go, or is precious group time spent in setting up equipment? Is the group starting 20 minutes later than you planned? Were you realistic about the announced time for the meeting? Does it really need to start later? If food is being served, is that process smooth and appropriately timed? How much time is spent reading and approving previous minutes? Would it be possible to have those minutes sent in advance of the meeting for comments and corrections? Could any of the reports be sent and considered in advance of the meeting? Do the reports give the kind of information that helps the group? Are there other ways to communicate helpfully?

Ask God for guidance in communicating with any people who need to be contacted before the meeting. Everyone processes change differently. Everyone has different needs and attachments to organizational decisions. Some folks need to talk things out; some need to mull things over internally. There are procedures and processes to honor. People want to know that others respect them and consider their needs.

Consider some additional details in preparing for meetings:

Always consult those charged with overseeing and implementing the task, decision, or issue. It is common sense not to bring a proposal for a library auction without consulting the librarian and the chair of the library's oversight committee. It might also be wise to speak with those folks who have used the library the most. Check the ideas with the people who do the work and receive the services; this can save you and the group time and grief.

Remember to give every person who has responsibility for this issue a "heads up." It is deadly for group process to consult with some of the pertinent individuals and omit others.

For instance, if the education committee proposes starting a program for the needs of the migrant community, you should make sure that every part of the organization affected by this program would be "in the loop." The worship planners might not have thought of the bilingual needs this would present for worship. The classroom teachers in the Christian education program may not have thought about the bilingual needs in their classrooms. The Peace and Justice Committee might be working on parallel concerns and would have important input. It isn't necessary or even desirable for the clerk to have all these conversations, but it is the clerk's responsibility to think about and facilitate these connections. If these interfaces are not made *before* the proposal comes to the meeting, a good bit of meeting time will be wasted in discussion.

Honor personal investments, personality styles, and handicaps. If you know that the furniture in the fellowship hall was given in memory of Grandpa Jones, talk with the family before you place on the agenda a remodeling plan that would require removing the furniture. If you know someone always acts out if she is caught by surprise, don't surprise her. If some have trouble following a group discussion because of hearing loss, make provision for those needs. In short, the goal of the clerk is to create the space in which each participant can be his or her best self.

Pre-Meeting Checklist

☐ Make sure you are spiritually prepared for the meeting.

☐ Divide the task into manageable chunks to aid in the group's decision-making process.

☐ Think through the flow of the task. If it would be useful, make a flow chart.

☐ Decide what information the group needs.

☐ Determine the best way to communicate this information. Prepare the information.

☐ Communicate with the appropriate people so they know what will be coming to the group for discernment.

☐ Check the timelines to see that you have sufficient time and space to make good decisions. In volunteer organizations, check the availability of key players.

☐ Plan or arrange for worship to begin the meeting.

☐ Hold the group in prayer, that its members will be able to discern God's leadings.

You are ready for the meeting!

6

THE LEADER PRESENTS THE ISSUES AND GUIDES THE DISCUSSION

Jan Wood

Listening to God as a group has a paradoxical quality to it. On the one hand, the process goes best when each person is fully prepared. A good bit of thinking, praying, listening, and planning already has gone into the process by the time the group gathers.

Yet once we get to the meeting, we all agree to lay down our preconceived notions, ideas, and even convictions, and to allow God to perceptibly move among us. One of the best ways to lay down our plans and agendas and kneel before the sovereignty of our Lord is through worship. This is not a perfunctory Scripture reading, song, or prayer for guidance. It is a time of bona fide worship that brings all into the presence of God. Business is done in the spirit of worship.

The shape of this worship will be unique to your organization. A congregation might come into worship through singing Scripture songs for ten minutes. Another Christian organization might find it more helpful to have several minutes of silence to center and focus. Choose the form of worship based on your assessment of how you best honor God in your group. Again, this is not waving a pious wand over the proceedings; it is truly entering into the knowledge that God is present and active, here and now.

Presenting the Issue

As you prepare to present the issue to the group, keep in mind several important issues that will facilitate the meeting.

1. Give appropriate background information. Start with the narrative of the group's process to this point. The group needs to hear how God has worked so far. This storytelling is very important. It might sound something like this:

> We knew that we had outgrown this building, but we were not at all sure if we should demolish the present structure and rebuild on this property or sell this property and build in another location. We knew that we didn't want to leave this neighborhood without a Christian witness and fellowship. But as we were trying to decide, a Korean congregation approached us about buying our building. As we considered that, it seemed good and right to us all that we pass our ministry and mission in this neighborhood to them and that we should build in another location. Today we are considering a report from the trustees on three different parcels of land that we might purchase. Each would present new opportunities and new challenges.

If a committee already has spent time sorting out the issues and answering the questions, summarize the process the committee has gone through. It is not appropriate to simply say that the committee has spent many hours working on this, implying that this is the only right answer. Trace the work of the committee for the larger group so that everyone can see how the committee thought about the important issues; many of these discussions don't need to be duplicated in the larger group. Bring the group in on the thoroughness and thoughtfulness of the committee's process!

The building committee realized that just because a piece of property was available to us didn't mean that it was wise of us to relocate there. First we asked the question, "What is our mission?" We knew we had a history of being a neighborhood church. We wouldn't be able to do what we do best if we were sitting in the middle of a cornfield. We then asked ourselves how important visibility is to our location. It would be much more expensive to acquire property on a main thoroughfare; but would our church's school be enhanced by good visibility and access? We were mindful of our heart for children and youth ministries, so we also knew that we would need to find out the demographics of any neighborhood to which we would consider moving.

We have brought these three properties for your consideration. Each of them meets our criteria of mission, accessibility, demographics, and zoning requirements. We met with the other churches in the neighborhoods we are considering, to find out what ministries are already flourishing and where there are needs our congregation can meet. Each property presents some significant opportunities and challenges, which are described in the PowerPoint presentation we have prepared for you.

2. Clarify what the group is being asked to discern. Present the specific issue and make clear the expectation for the group discernment. It may be that you have a specific proposal to approve.

We are proposing that we contract with Goodfellow Construction Company. We would authorize Miriam D'Much to be our representative in these transactions. The trustees will furnish the congregation with a monthly progress report. This contract needs congregational approval.

If some discussion needs to take place, but no decision is to be made, make that clear.

> The Christian Education Committee has been concerned about the needs of the migrant children in our area. We don't know what we can or should do, but we would like the group to seek God's guidance about our redemptive role in this community. We aren't asking for a decision today. We just want to start the listening process.

3. Present the information that empowers the group to listen well. The whole group needs to have adequate information. In many cases, the information is not complex and can be communicated verbally. At other times it helps to have it written, so that people can both hear it and read it. Handouts, overhead transparencies, or PowerPoint presentations will help in sharing necessary information. And remember, creativity and humor are the communicator's best friends.

4. Explain what the group brings to the process. Groups can find themselves tangled in the underbrush of unstated perceptions and emotions that trip up otherwise sound processes. It helps a great deal to acknowledge the truth of the matter. Consider a few ways the clerk might frame the issue.

- The truth is we have tried to talk about this before— but we are hopelessly divided. We aren't even sure if we would recognize what God might say.

- The truth is we aren't even sure that we can all listen together. Some of us are pretty skeptical.

- The truth is that we have wounded one another badly in this congregation. We don't trust each other. We are afraid to make ourselves vulnerable to this process.

- The truth is that the task is so big and we don't see how we could possibly have the resources to do it.

- The truth is we are raring to go—but we have so many great ideas we don't know where to start and how to prioritize our resources.

- The truth is we are good at starting things, but we don't keep them up very well.

5. Go into silence, listening, and waiting. Give God a chance to communicate. Often we talk about listening to God, but we don't give God a chance to get any words in edgewise. Give God the same listening courtesies that you would give to anyone else. Be attentive. Be quiet. Receive.

As clerk you may need to give some instructions about how participants do this listening in the silence. Even those familiar with the process can use a reminder every now and then!

6. Encourage participants to release all the thoughts filling their minds. This releasing of thoughts includes laying aside concerns not germane to this meeting. It includes all the ideas and opinions we have brought into this meeting.

7. Make sure the group is holding each participant in respect. Direct participants to release their judgments about each person into Jesus' hands, even if they feel absolutely sure these individuals can't "hear" God or wouldn't listen if they did. Say something like, "Forgive anyone who has wounded us in the group."

8. Become silent inside and out. It may help to imagine yourself telling Jesus all about it or just handing him the proposal or issue. Then simply observe the thoughts, feelings, and sensations that come to you or rise up within you. As Bruce

Bishop described in chapter 2, God communicates through these nudges, thoughts, images, and sensations. Rarely is any one of them complete, but together they make a whole. How delightful that God honors all of us with a piece of the process!

Ready for the Next Step

In the following chapter we will explore the process of speaking out of the silence, which can be an amazing and rewarding process. Then we gather together the results of God's speaking.

As humans, we each hear God in a different way, but only one God does the speaking. So we look forward to melding the results of our different listening perspectives.

7

THE LEADER FACILITATES THE DECISION-MAKING PROCESS

Jan Wood

Moving forward from the time of waiting in silence before the Lord, the clerk should simply ask people to share what came to them in listening to God. Phrasing the invitation in this way helps to get away from the framework of debate so typical of group decision making.

In a small and informal group, it may be sufficient for each person to speak out of a period of silence. The clerk may intervene, however, if the group shifts from listening to discussing or arguing; or if the participants do not allow for silence so that each person's leading can be received and considered by the group.

In a large group, the clerk will need to recognize each speaker when it comes to that person's time to speak. Whether this is done by queuing up to a microphone, by standing, or by raising one's hand, the speaker waits until the clerk acknowledges him or her. And the clerk allows for some time between messages for worshipful listening. In this way the clerk can guide the pace of the process. And in general, the clerk calls upon people to speak in the order in which they indicated their desire to speak. The participants might express themselves like this:

- "This Scripture came to me so strongly…."
- "I kept wondering what would happen if…."
- "I had this sense that Jesus was smiling."
- "I think this proposal is in violation of our bylaws."
- "I felt myself getting really uncomfortable and felt irritated. I think something is not quite right with this proposal yet."
- "I had a knot in the pit of my stomach."

Don't panic because the things people are saying seem to conflict with one another! Don't ignore the negative-sounding statements. Don't automatically discount what sounds like an "inappropriate" comment because of someone's age, lack of social skills, inarticulateness, or strong emotions. Simply let all these statements come out and rest on the proverbial table in the middle of the room. They are all part of the unfolding of God's guidance, like the scattered pieces of a jigsaw puzzle before the puzzle gets assembled.

Usually the clerk makes no comment on what has been offered. There may be exceptions to that, however.

- If the contributions become tangential to the purpose at hand, the clerk needs to refocus the group on the stated issue to be discerned.

- If the statements are important to the process but not part of the decision at hand, the clerk can note that and make provision for these new issues to be handled at a different time.

- If someone has spoken harshly or has verbally attacked a person or idea, the clerk may be able to summarize or reframe the comments so that the group can hear the meanings and good intentions underneath the emotional language. This is a way of gracing the speaker and clarifying the content.

- If someone has become lost in his or her words and has not been clear, a reflective question may clarify the contribution both for the speaker and the group.

- If a speaker has been speaking inordinately long, it may be necessary for the clerk to interrupt the speaker with a request that he or she draw the comments to a close.

- In smaller groups, there may be situations in which the clerk can see that a person has something to contribute but has not asked to be recognized or entered into the speaking. It is permissible for the clerk to call on that person to ask if he or she has something to say. Of course, the clerk should not insist that the person speak, if he or she does not feel so led.

Reflective Listening...to God

When the group has a sense that everyone who has something to offer has done so, the task moves into a gentle process of trial and error, the goal of which is to see the pattern of this. The clerk can start off this phase of the process by asking if anyone has a sense of how God is showing the way forward. Someone may say something like:

> I sense we are on the right track with this proposal, but there is a part of it about which we are not in unity. I am wondering if the dis-ease that some of you felt in the silence was about this part. Maybe that part needs to be adjusted to take account of....

The group lets a few moments of silence elapse to let this statement settle inside. Then another person might say,

> I was fine until we got to this section—and then I got this knot in my stomach. Maybe there is something we need to look at in that part.

There is no way to script how this will develop in the group. But the task is to begin to shape our possible leadings into words—and the group keeps testing them in an attitude of collaborative seeking. Even strong and opposing opinions are framed in the context of being *on the same side* searching for the leadings that will emerge from a God who loves us and wants to participate with us.

In many matters, the sense of the meeting will rise quickly. People will shape it with what they have perceived in the silence. And the decision gets made with full-hearted yes-ness. The group will feel deeply satisfied that God is present and partnering with them. In other matters, perspectives may arise that surprise the clerk and the group. There may be other information to gather, other factors to explore and consider. It then becomes necessary to do further homework and return to the decision-making process at another time.

When the group gets stuck with conflict or confusion, the clerk stops the process and leads the group into listening silence again. This time everyone simply holds the truth in prayer that the group seems stuck. People don't know how to proceed. At the end of the silence, the clerk asks if anyone was given the way forward. Usually that is exactly what has taken place. The stories are endless. Sometimes a flash of insight occurs and it all unfolds. Often we find we have been asking the wrong question or framing the issue inadequately.

One example of that came in a meeting for business in which the budget needed to be cut. None of the cuts were easy and some of them were downright painful. And the group got stuck. No one wanted to approve this budget, yet what else could they do?

The clerk called for listening silence, and new questions came out of that silence. "Is there anything in these budget cuts that would prevent any of us from being faithful?" As each person considered what they were called to do and if they could do it with these means, one by one each person agreed that they could be faithful under these constraints. And presto, the budget was approved with yes-ness and unity.

At other times we may not know the answer, but our hostile and fear-filled feelings melt away and we are able to give grace to people who think differently than we do. Some times we don't know the whole answer, but we do know the next step. It is human nature to get stuck in the differences and the points of disagreement. Our minds get stuck and can frame the issue in only one way. Whether we like it or not, we fall into win-lose thinking. The clerk can help the group by periodically restating what the group affirms that transcends the immediate disagreement. Recount where the Spirit has clearly led so far; name what remains true for everyone.

- "We don't know whether we are to continue this day care ministry, but we know that we all care deeply about these children and teachers."

- "While we are very divided about the wisdom of buying this property for the church, we are all clear that we have been led to build at a new location."

- "We struggled together to come to that decision. But we did come to unity."

- "We know that God wouldn't lead us this far and let us be fragmented now."

- "God will show us. If this is God's choice for us, it won't slip through our fingers while we are trying to be faithful."

The most important thing for the clerk to remember is that God can handle *any* moment! It is OK to not know. It is OK to labor together to acquire something important. It is OK to wait. Wait for people to respond in this meeting. Wait for another meeting.

Waiting

Waiting is not like tabling an action and avoiding the tough decisions. It may feel like defeat, as though we haven't done our work of listening to God. Nothing could be further from reality! Waiting in the presence of God is a full and active step that furthers the process of being guided—and this work does not always get accomplished in one sitting. Scriptures repeatedly lift up the spiritual discipline of waiting on God.

1. Personal Waiting. The period of waiting—be it a few minutes in the meeting or a few weeks between meetings—is a very active process of listening to ourselves and to God. Again, here we encounter a paradoxical truth. On the one hand, each person listens to the truth as he or she experiences and perceives it. In the waiting we can sense how scared or frustrated we feel. We can feel the textures of what rides on this decision for us and those we care about. We have a chance to figure out what lies underneath our flash of irritation and anger, the blanket of sadness, or our soaring hopefulness.

The waiting gives us the space to bring our personal reality into the presence of God. This may simply illuminate the issues being decided. But it may also be an opportunity for spiritual growth and healing.

> When Ted McBride said he didn't see any use for a ministry to street people because they would never support the work of the church, I went ballistic. I lost control

inside and out. In that moment I knew I hated Ted. I knew all the God reasons I feel so strongly about this outreach—but why was I out of control? Why did such anger and hatred rise up in me? I had to sit with God about this for quite a while. But then I remembered this incident when I was a teenager...

This is an example of God making us aware of a deep and negative memory that can be healed. We all have old wounds that have gone untended and unremembered, but that have never lost their toxicity. These unexpected "ouches" are gifts to us if we will be faithful to them. They reintroduce us to the experiences that can be healed here and now through God's love and presence.* Once we have experienced that joyous release from the old pain, we realize our opponent may still be "wrong," but we can hold her or him in love. Amazingly, not only can we release the person from our judgment, we can rejoice because even that person's "wrongness" worked together for our good. It really is true that all things work together for good!

The other side of the paradoxical task of reflecting on the differences in the group is that we again surrender to the lordship of Christ and Christ's guidance *in full awareness* of our needs, preferences, convictions, and even our understandings of Scripture or prophetic knowings. *Everything* is released continuously into the hand of God. Sometimes we are so sure we are right that it is very difficult to release that "rightness" to God again and again. But if we are right, then the power of God is behind us; we need not push, bully, politick, or manipulate. We can afford to be faithful to word and action—and let God do with that as God wishes. If we are *not* right, we

---

* There are many fine books on the process of receiving healing for past wounds, e.g., Prayer, Stress, and Our Inner Wounds, by Flora Slosson Wuellner (Nashville: Upper Room, 1985).

certainly wouldn't want to fight God through our inclinations to push, bully, or manipulate in opposition to the leadings of God. We really would not want to become like Saul of Tarsus, who discovered he was pushing the wrong agenda (see Acts 9).

The easiest thing to do is to talk only with people who agree with us. It is much harder (and more rewarding!) to work at understanding those who disagree with us. Be that as it may, the waiting is an opportunity. It is not the time or place to try to convince others of our viewpoint. Great good can emerge, however, when we ask others to tell us why they see this issue the way they do. Our disagreement may not go away, but this kind of communication usually develops respect and understanding. And this respect is fertile ground for God's love and guidance to flourish.

Thus our personal waiting is a space in which God's Spirit can act upon us. We take note of what rises within us as we hold this issue in our thoughts and prayers. We pay attention to things that come to us—scriptures, things we hear or read, conversations we have, situations we encounter. We don't have to work to "make something happen," but we do remain faithful to find ways to understand those who think differently than we do. And we quietly live out of a receptive space in our thinking, feeling, and spirit.

2. Group Waiting. As clerk you can take several steps to help your group wait more effectively in various circumstances.

• *Wait within the meeting to refocus or hear God more clearly.*

Within the meeting, it is often wise to stop and wait. This gives the group a chance to catch its collective breath, recenter, and listen to the whispers of God's leadings. This waiting can be as long or as short as it needs to be to facilitate the next steps of sharing and discerning.

• *Wait until another meeting for further information.*

Sometimes the group needs to end the meeting and wait until another meeting to continue consideration of the issue. If the decision to wait hinges on the lack of complete information, this is straightforward. More homework needs to be done, options explored more fully, ideas researched, details attended to. The clerk, of course, can facilitate the assignment of tasks.

• *Wait in the face of disagreement.*

If the decision to wait has come out of entrenched disagreement, the clerk may wish to structure some interactions during the waiting. Often, listening meetings are productive, as discussed in our case study about the church with a day care ministry.

Listening meetings are called for the sole purpose of listening to one another. Here are the ground rules: No decision or recommendation will be made in this gathering; each person has the opportunity to declare what he or she is thinking, feeling, and perceiving. No questions are allowed except questions for clarification. No one discusses what people are saying. Each person is simply listened to, and their thoughts received. Customarily some silence separates the speakers. It is best to appoint a facilitator who helps to clarify the purpose and ground rules of the meeting, to gently pull people back if the process breaks down, and to close the meeting at the appointed time. In our case study regarding the day care program, you will notice that this church had weekly listening meetings for a month while they remained in their waiting process.

During the Waiting

In some situations, disagreements may feel deeply wounding or disturbing to some individuals. The clerk may need to make sure he or she has mature people who can walk alongside those people who are troubled—laboring with them in their process, listening and doing the tug and pull that clarifies and releases, helping the healing and forgiving where appropriate, praying. Conflict can be an occasion of great spiritual growth, but this rarely happens in solitude. Most people need someone to love them and walk with them as they take those next steps.

The clerk may be especially aware of those individuals with prophetic gifts, often the odd-person-out in the process. Their voices may seem too impractical, too impassioned, and too oppositional. The prophets among us often feel afraid and unrecognized. Again, the clerk may want to make sure that he or she has mature individuals present, willing to walk alongside those who may speak a truth painfully out-of-step with the group. Those who try to remain faithful to their prophetic gift have many questions!

> No one seems to understand that this message is from God—what should I do? What if it isn't from God, but just my own strong opinion? What if it is from God and I chickened out? Is this a seed that will grow and I should just be faithful in those things I can do and release the group? Or is it faithfulness to be more forceful? Do I stand aside or do I block a decision that I sense is not "it"?

Prophets need discerners. The waiting allows time for mentors and discerners to be in process with the prophets.

8

CONCLUDING THE DECISION MAKING

Jan Wood

Now the group must move from waiting and processing the results of hearing God's voice to making a decision. Anyone can ask if the group has come to a sense of the meeting. But more often than not, the clerk senses when the group has moved close to a decision.

Various signs indicate that the group has become ready to decide. Often all dissent vanishes. The matter has been brought before the group, all information relayed, the decision seems good to the group, and no lengthy process is necessary (or a lengthy process has come to a definitive conclusion). Now the clerk asks, "Do I sense agreement with this recommendation?"

In other situations, people may still have much to say, but the clerk has noticed a shift from making the decision to implementing the decision:

> I am hearing that we have lots of good ideas about how the soup kitchen could be run. But under all this, I sense that we are ready to approve the concept of starting a soup kitchen. Do we have approval?

In divisive situations, the clerk may not know where the group stands. Or it may seem clear that most folks feel ready to approve, but a distinct person or minority remains in disagreement. The clerk can proceed in one of several ways. He or she can ask the group where it is:

> I'm having a hard time discerning where we are. What is the leading of the group in this matter?

The clerk can state his or her observation:

> My sense of God's working among us is that many are ready to proceed with this proposal. Several others have deep reservations. Are these reservations that should stop our action or are they reservations that we should simply be mindful of as we proceed?

The clerk can also reframe the issue:

> We seemed to be divided over what action is faithfulness for us in light of the impending war. Yet I see that we all care deeply about being biblically faithful. We all care for our country and want to be helpful citizens. Are we stuck in one way of looking at the issue? Are there things that we can be in unity around? Or are there some steps that we all feel clear to proceed upon?

Completing the Decision

The group arrives at a decision when the clerk names the decision and the group gives verbal approval. Not every decision has to be the final resolution of the issue, and recognizing this can be very helpful. Decisions need not conclude the process.

Some decisions are easy to name; the clerk can quickly sense movement toward agreement:

> The Smith family has requested membership. They have met with the elders who have recommended our acceptance with joy. Are we clear to accept this membership request?

The treasurer's report indicates that we have a startling shortfall of contributions each August. It has been suggested that Matt Fine and Betty Good work on some creative, lighthearted promotional material that can help us all plan ahead for our summer giving. We don't want to give our treasurer gray hairs every August! Do I sense that this suggestion meets with our approval?

Some difficult decisions may take much time and energy to arrive at, but they are clear:

I sense that we are now ready to accept the proposal for the relocation of the church. Are we clear to approve?

Sometimes the group does not know the final resolution, but it does know the next step. The decision articulates that next step:

We don't know what the shape of our ministry to the migrant community is supposed to be. But we do know we have a heart for this community and want to start assessing the needs and how we might address them. I am hearing that we are to appoint an exploratory committee to seek out information. Do we have agreement to form an exploratory committee? Can we name the members of this committee?

It appears that we have significant differences among us. We know where each person stands, but we don't know why each person feels so strongly in his or her position. Would it be wise for us to schedule two listening meetings between now and the next business meeting so that we can fully respect and consider each other's thinking?

This concern came to us as a "should." Yet we have not been able to find any sense of yes-ness in all the discussing and listening we have done. Perhaps we are to simply drop it, and if God wants us involved, it will rise again with more clarity. Does that seem to be the way forward?

When the Group Is Not United

In most cases, decisions made by group discernment are reasonably easy to recognize by a sense of clarity in the group that the way forward has been found. Sometimes, however, when the clerk asks if the group can unite on a decision, it becomes clear that while most of the group can, one or more exceptions exist. At that point the clerk must make a crucial discernment call.

- Does the clerk sense that those without clarity are expressing an authentic check of the Spirit, regardless of how enthusiastic the rest of the group is for this proposal? If so, the clerk may postpone the decision and suggest appropriate interim actions (e.g., listening meetings or further prayer).

- Does the clerk feel that the group truly has been guided by God's wisdom and that these objections do not alter that reality? In that case, the clerk can state that the group as a whole seems to be sensing the yes-ness of God's spirit in this matter, yet person "A" and person "B" are not clear to unite. The clerk may then choose to ask them if they would be clear to stand aside and let the decision go forward. If so, the decision proceeds, with the dissenting individuals putting their trust in the greater discernment of the group. The people's standing aside can be noted in the final minute, if those people so choose.

Occasionally the individual may not feel clear about standing aside if the group continues to move forward despite the objections. In that case, it *is* possible for the clerk to move ahead despite the objection, even though that would be a rare situation. In that case, the resulting minute might indicate that the person was "unable to unite" with the decision. In such a situation, the dissenting individual has been unable to trust the discernment of the meeting. This broken trust causes a rift—a wound that needs to be healed with diligent effort on the part of all parties. The goal is for the dissenting individual to once again become spiritually and emotionally free to participate in group discernment.

Recording the Decision

The Quaker system of listening has a very helpful component. Rather than having a secretary, Quakers use what is called a "recording clerk." Whereas a traditional secretary writes the minutes to be approved at the following meeting, the recording clerk (possibly with the help of the presiding clerk) writes the minute at the conclusion of each decision process.

If necessary, the group waits in silence while the recording clerk captures the sense of the leading in the minute. Then the minute is read back to the group to see if it accurately reflects the decision. If the group does not agree that the minute has captured the sense of the meeting, then the recording clerk and presiding clerk make revisions while the group upholds them in the silence. This process continues until the written minute matches both the accuracy and spirit of the agreed-upon decision.

Minutes may be very straightforward or very complex. The ordinary minute would state only the decision:

> The transfer of membership of John and Clara Brown to Indianapolis Community Church was approved. Our blessings and prayers go with them.

Just as often, the group has come to a sense of the meeting, yet significant issues have been raised in the process of working through differences. In these cases, the minute can be very helpful by acknowledging the process:

> The proposal from the trustees to relocate the church was approved. As we labored with this decision over the last three months, we struggled together to know if our ministry in this community was completed. We grieved together at the thought of leaving the building and grounds in which so many dear folks have invested their lives and energies over the years. But we felt Christ's guidance when the Korean congregation approached us about buying our building. We know that we will be leaving this community in good hands. And it is with a sense of anticipation that we are agreed to take these next steps.

> The Pastoral Search Committee presented its recommendation to call Jane Brown as senior pastor for a three-year period effective July 1, ___. While her credentials are superb and our congregational interactions have been very confirming, there was hesitation on the part of some about whether it was biblical to have a woman pastor. We listened together about the concern for biblical soundness. While everyone could not be in unity with the call, the sense of the meeting was that we were to proceed with the call to Jane Brown. The three-year call, effective, July 1, ___ was approved with Jason Highweather standing aside.

When the group decides to wait until another time to take definitive action, a minute very helpfully provides the context for resuming the discussion later. The minute of process lets the group feel heard. It documents the flow of the concerns so that these concerns do not have to be repeated at the next meeting. It lets future generations understand the process the group went through to reach the final decision:

> We are unable to come to unity over the proposed change in the Yearly Meeting Discipline regarding the issue of abortion. We are deeply divided between those who would identify themselves as pro-life and pro-choice. The spirit of our listening together has been passionate and respectful. We are united in our love and concern for mothers and babies, but we are not in agreement about how we express that. Thus we are in agreement to wait for further leading. The Family Life Committee has agreed to set up some listening meetings over the next month to allow us to share our concerns with one another more deeply. A member of the Yearly Meeting Family Life Board will meet with us on October 4 to share the leadings of the board. We will hold these issues in prayer as we seek guidance.

Clerk as Coach

The clerk facilitates a collaborative process. The giftedness and skills of a clerk are as important to the group as a coach is to an athletic team. Yet the responsibility for the decision does not rest upon the shoulders of the clerk, for it is God who makes known the decisions and next steps. The clerk does not control the content or the outcome of the meeting, yet he or she does maximize the conditions under which people can work helpfully together.

Elements of group discernment are applicable to various settings. They may appear different in a college or business setting, but it is always possible to lead people into seeking God's wisdom in tangible and collaborative ways.

It is not essential, of course, that the leader of group discernment be called a clerk. The titles of president, moderator, chairperson, or CEO are perfectly OK. You may be operating within the constraints of Robert's Rules of Order. Yet it is possible to incorporate the spirit of clerking that liberates God's wisdom to be known. For those of us whose polity is based on group discernment, the invitation is always to go beyond the forms and procedures to the life and power that undergird them.

Checklist for the Meeting for Business

☐ Worship

☐ Approval of previous minutes

☐ Presentation of issue

☐ Group listening in silence

☐ Sharing what the group is perceiving

☐ Shifting into collaborative understanding of how these perceptions are fitting together

☐ Naming the emerging decision/next step

☐ Writing a provisional minute

☐ Adjustment of the minute for accuracy of content and of spirit

☐ If clear, approval of the minute

☐ Recording the minute and its approval

☐ If not clear, articulation of when the issue will be revisited and what steps are to be taken in the intervening time

☐ Expression of thanksgiving for God's work!

Checklist for After the Meeting

☐ Follow through on any action items requiring implementation

☐ Letters to be written; documents to be signed

☐ Necessary communication with people/committees

☐ Further meetings to be scheduled

☐ Notes/e-mails of appreciation

☐ Follow-up conversations that might be wise

GROUP SPIRITUAL DISCERNMENT
ON THE REGIONAL LEVEL

You could almost feel the excitement and anticipation for what God might have in store for this Northwest church denomination of some seven thousand members. On the one hand, members rejoiced that 80 years of missions work in Bolivia and Peru had borne much fruit. Mature, self-governing churches had arisen among the Aymara people; they no longer had a need for full-time missionaries. On the other hand, the missions work had been very important to many people and many felt a sense of loss over the closing of the missionary work in these countries.

The members certainly wanted to continue to be faithful to mission work that still needed to be done elsewhere in the world, so a survey team had been commissioned to explore several possible new fields for evangelism. Would they uncover the next new focus for sharing the good news of Christ?

The survey team presented preliminary reports, using the imagery of the Numbers 13 exploration of the Promised Land by the Israelites. They found good potential, exciting possibilities, and people who seemed spiritually hungry. The excitement for a new missionary movement began to blossom as people were asked to pray together and prepare to hear God's leading at the annual sessions that summer.

In July, the people gathered amid much excitement. Nearly five hundred people attended the annual gathering, representing each of the denomination's churches from Oregon, Idaho, and Washington. They had the opportunity to seek the mind of the Lord about where to focus the next call to evangelism. One could feel the crowd's energy. A new venture and a new focus. A new, fresh call in being the people of God!

The survey team presented its report, reading Scripture in the language of the people group under discussion. The recommendation was made: "The Board of Missions requests approval and endorsement for the beginning of a cross-cultural service, witness, and evangelism program in North Africa."

The clerk opened the meeting for response. Many spoke of their excitement about this new venture. And then something unexpected happened: A local church representative stood and read a letter from her church, expressing concern that the focus of the proposal seemed to exclude evangelism within the United States. She then shared the following statement from their local church minutes:

> The meeting discussed a concern that some fields might require "stealth operations," i.e., where workers would be required to work in secret—not openly professing their faith or purpose. The meeting agreed that such an approach is not consistent with the direct and truthful way the denomination has been called to present Christ.

After the reading of this minute, many people felt that a cold wave had filled the room. The excitement and energy dissipated and in its place came disappointment and tension. How could *anyone* question the call into a new mission field? The concern centered on the issue of sending missionaries to a place where Christian mission work was illegal. Those who went would be "tentmakers," engaged in an acceptable vocation. But the mission board had proposed that these people would secretly function as missionaries. Expectations for them would be similar to those for missionaries elsewhere.

The local church that was raising the concern expressed apprehension over something they considered to be deceptive and possibly illegal. Could the denomination, with integrity, minister in such a way? Was honesty not at the heart of what it meant to follow Christ? The meeting waited in silence. Then a few expressed strong feelings that human spiritual needs overruled the anti-Christian laws of a particular country. The people *needed* to hear the gospel! The discussion moved back and forth between the historical testimony of integrity and the need to evangelize a spiritually hungry people.

Once again, a feeling of despair seemed to fill the room. How could a group of five hundred people, from widespread locations around the Northwest, find a way forward when it appeared two important values conflicted with each other? Would the decision need to be postponed for another year, while it was discussed in local churches and the way forward sought? Could the sense of the meeting be found in such a situation?

The morning break arrived, pushing what was thought to be a quick affirmation into a new session of business. After the break, the clerk called for a time of prayerful silence, with the admonition that participants make an effort to create space to hear from God by laying aside preferences and preconceptions. Then verbal prayers were invited, resulting in a common theme: The people desired to hear and obey the leading of God.

After the prayer time, discussion resumed. People gave strong expressions about maintaining integrity *and* pursuing evangelistic relationships. The clerk then asked for space to work with the assistant clerk on new wording for the original minute. He encouraged the people to prayerfully support this process. The spirit in the room remained still and heavy. How could such an opportunity for evangelism be ignored? And yet, how could truth be compromised for evangelism's sake?

Into the silence, the clerk read the following minute:

> **The Board of Missions proposes that we support and encourage those of us who are called by God to be followers of Christ as they live and work…in North Africa.**

A collective sigh and sense of leading swept the room. This would work! It affirmed the desire to share Christ, but was upfront about sending Christlike individuals to live and work among the people, rather than secretly sending outlawed missionaries. The minute affirmed both values! Many would have been ready to approve the minute at that moment, but the clerk asked everyone to prayerfully consider the new minute until the following morning's business session.

That next morning, the clerk reopened consideration of the new recommendation. Several spoke to their sense of joy and completeness with the wording of the new minute. It not only maintained the church's integrity, but it also pointed in a new direction for the entire missions effort. Instead of simply relying on traditional or professional missionaries, the church was affirming the need for individuals to be the sort of Christ-followers that spread Christ's light as they lived and worked. This was a challenge for *every member* of the denomination to consider for their own spheres of influence—and it was a joy to be able to release some people to do it overseas.

The clerk reread the minute and asked for a time of quiet waiting to discern God's will. After his question, all members approved the new recommendation with joy and conviction. No one felt the need to hold back or feel overruled. No one would go home with misgivings. Instead, the Board of Missions had received a new definition of evangelism to carry them into the new century, and each individual had been prompted to consider the shape of his or her own life and ministry. For isn't *each of us* called to be a follower of Christ as we live and work among people?

God indeed had provided a way forward, even though it looked different from what had been expected. By considering the input of different members and different perspectives, people saw the bigger picture that God desired to reveal.

epilogue

DECISION MAKING AS A WITNESS TO THE WORLD

God's love sent Jesus to teach us and make provision for our sinful nature and the deep wounds of the human condition. Everyone can be saved and liberated from the bondages that prevent us from becoming our God-begotten selves. But the good news doesn't end there.

God sent God's very own Spirit to dwell within each believer to teach, guide, and lead. This indwelling presence of the Holy brings interlocking giftedness to the people of God. This enables us to arrange ourselves in new and radical ways that witness to the world that Jesus is Lord and the reign of God has begun on earth.

The world's system insists that the only way to make effective decisions is to follow orders or to be a voting body. The world's methods amount to either coercion or politicking. The authors bear witness to a biblical method of making decisions that transcends these ways of doing business—in families, churches, organizations, and businesses.

Decision making through discernment rejects the creation of "us" and "them." We all stand together on one side, listening together for the voice of God among us.

Decision making through discernment rejects the demonizing of those with whom we disagree or those we find ourselves fearing. It refuses to make an enemy of anyone God loves. It refuses to wound a sister or brother with harsh words or rhetoric.

Group discernment transcends the need to play politics, persuade others to our views, or engage in battles over the interpretation of Scripture verses. It refuses to marginalize those who stand in a different place, as they too are listening. It offers grace and a constant space of forgiveness for those who can't listen well for some reason.

As those of us who have experienced the wonder and joy of this process can attest, decisions arrived at by discernment truly witness to the fact that God is God and that faithfulness is an amazing journey. We know the joy of being surprised by God's opening the way through the "Red Seas" of the no-win situations we face together as Christians. We know how natural it is to walk in humility when we have experienced the visible hand of God among us. We know how sturdy relationships can become when we commit ourselves to listening together.

We have learned not merely to talk grace and forgiveness, but we know how it feels to extend such grace and forgiveness to others as an undergirding stream. We have learned how it feels to be washed in grace and forgiveness when we have been the ones off base. We have learned to respect people we normally would have judged and belittled. We know how fruitful God-given decisions can be as we remain faithful to them. We have joyfully seen the words of Scripture come alive from the inside out as the Holy Spirit created a new arrangement in our churches and organizations.

Our faith that God is with us *all the time* has become grounded in real experience; we have learned how God looks and acts in the "real world." And when people shake their heads and tell us it is amazing that a group could operate like this, we know that we truly are witnesses that the kingdom has come, on earth as it is in heaven.

GLOSSARY

Clearness: Early Quakers had "meetings for clearness"; some still follow this practice today. On one level, the meaning of clearness is the same as clarity, but there is a richer meaning that indicates the absence of any hindrance to discernment, inwardly or outwardly. Individually and in groups, we come to clearness by the patient process of discernment of the Holy Spirit's leading.

Clerk, Clerking: All sorts of words are used for those who lead groups and are in charge of decision-making meetings— e.g., *president*, *chair*, and *moderator*. We have taken the term *clerk* from the traditional Quaker word for the presiding officer. As expressed in this book, the leadership of the clerk is a spiritual exercise, a very different process from serving as chairman.

Consensus: This term means a process of coming to agreement in a group about an issue, usually by discussing, listening, and shaping an acceptable agreement. We have chosen not to use the term, preferring the stronger spiritual content of the word *discernment*. We are convinced that consensus is not an adequate process for groups of Christian believers, whose great challenge and opportunity is to discern God's leading.

Gathered Meeting: This is a term that was used among early Quakers. It means more than a group of people meeting together for worship or business. The *gathering* term refers to a keen consciousness of being gathered into the presence of the Holy Spirit. It is acknowledging that the Holy Spirit has moved in the meeting and thus the decisions arrived at aren't subject to political pressure from people not gathered (participating).

Listening Meeting: The purpose of a listening meeting is to listen carefully to the members of the group and to the Holy Spirit speaking through them. Some have called this a *threshing meeting*, referring to the threshing process from biblical times, in which grain was separated from chaff. It is made clear that no decision is to be made at the meeting. Members are invited to speak about their thoughts, feelings, fears, desires, and hopes without needing to defend the validity of these expressions.

Listen Under: This refers to seeking to discern what is "under" the words, emotions, and conflicts that others are expressing. The assumption is that under these things is to be found God's voice, ready to be uncovered and understood. It also means that one can listen to the heart and intent of another person rather than be limited by the language used.

Minute: Most organized groups that have business meetings designate a secretary to record the minutes of the discussion and action. The singular word *minute* is not normally used, but some Quakers speak of a minute as the individual statement capturing the discussion and the action that follows the discernment process.

Prayer of *Examen*: The "prayer of *examen*" mentioned in chapter 2 was originally developed by St. Ignatius of Loyola (see Tad Dunne, *Spiritual Exercises for Today: A Contemporary Presentation of the Classic Spiritual Exercises of Ignatius Loyola,* San Francisco: Harper San Francisco, 1991). Many spiritual leaders have refined the practice since Loyola first put it into words. The prayer of examen is an exercise in which we reflect on the past and ask Christ to walk with us through our memories and to first identify the "consolations"—the times when we were drawn closer to God. Then we are to identify and reflect on our "desolations"—the times we felt distant from God. Often we find consoling aspects to our experiences of desolation.

Sense of the Meeting: Quakers sometimes use this term in preference to *consensus,* indicating the understanding that emerges from waiting on God for leading. In its appropriate context, it recognizes that people have been meeting with God, not just with each other. A deeper level of spirituality is involved than the term *consensus* can indicate.

Standing Aside: Although sometimes misused as a way of trying to block action, at its best standing aside is a position taken by someone not yet in unity with the proposed action of the group. Standing aside acknowledges one's own misgivings about the action, but invites the group to proceed in the direction they are being led.

Unable to Unite: This is an option to be used carefully when a person feels very strongly that the group is in error in its proposed action and does not feel clear about standing aside. The person with this conviction presents his or her concern, gives the reasons, and asks that the group not move forward on this action. If the group feels led to continue forward in spite of the objections expressed, the one unable to unite may ask that his or her position be noted in the meeting minutes. In this situation, the dissenting individual has been unable to trust the discernment of the group. This broken trust causes a rift—a wound that must be healed before the dissenting individual will once again be spiritually and emotionally free to participate in group discernment.

Way Forward: This term points to the central process of discerning a position around which the group can unite and proceed in faithfulness. Important ingredients of this process are clarity about being led by God and coming to unity about that leading.

Weightiness: Spiritual maturity and experience provide particular strength to the voice of some people. This might be a general quality of wisdom that applies to most issues and may also apply to particular issues in which a weighty person has unusually helpful experience and sensitivity.

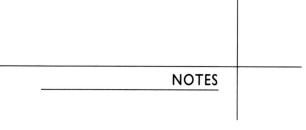

NOTES

Chapter 2

1. Frank Laubach, *Letters by a Modern Mystic* (Syracuse, New York: New York Readers Press, 1979), pp. 18-19.

2. Thomas R. Kelly, *A Testament of Devotion* (New York: Harper & Brothers, 1941), p. 35.

3. Dallas Willard, *The Spirit of the Disciplines: Understanding how God Changes Lives* (New York: HarperCollins, 1991), pp. 24-32.

Chapter 3

1. Thomas Kelly, *The Eternal Promise* (Richmond, Indiana: Friends United Press, 1977, 1988, 2006), p. 51.

Chapter 4

1. Kelly, *Eternal Promise*, p. 47.

FREQUENTLY ASKED QUESTIONS

*about the individual's part
in group discernment*

1. How do we deal with fear in the discernment process?
We know that "perfect love drives out fear," as the apostle John put it (1 John 4:18). But the problem is that our love is not always perfect. Our humanness takes over and we become fearful of the consequences of decisions.

Fear can actually be a helpful emotion to keep us from embracing foolish proposals. A number of Christian organizations have lost large amounts of money by placing their trust in dishonest individuals who offered lavish returns from shaky investment schemes. Their leaders needed to exercise more skepticism and greater fear that something too good to be true may be neither good nor true.

Disabling fear of the unknown, however, is the kind that kept the Hebrews wandering in the desert for 40 years. They felt afraid of the enemy's armies and they forgot God's many assurances that God would protect them and bring them safely to their destination.

Christian organizations face the unknown many times. It may be a change of leadership, a funding shortfall, or a change in circumstances that requires a different strategy of ministry. As individuals participating in the discernment process, we must name the group's fears and point to the many promises in

Scripture, such as: "So do not fear, for I am with you; do not be dismayed, for I am your God. I will strengthen you and help you; I will uphold you with my righteous right hand" (Isaiah 41:10).

2. How does anger affect group discernment? Some people have an internal thermostat that goes up rapidly and visibly when they get angry. Their neck and face become red and in extreme cases the whole body begins shaking. Those around them have to find a way to defuse the situation or simply let the person vent before the discussion can proceed.

Most of us aren't afflicted with such a short fuse. But if we were honest, we would admit that others do and say things that make us angry. Anger can be a helpful emotion. It signals that something isn't what you wanted or needed.

Anger needs to be acknowledged and listened to. It holds important information. But once its message has been delivered, we are wise to release the angry feelings that brought the issue to our attention. If we hold and give fuel to the angry feelings, those feelings cloud our judgment, stand in the way of our hearing what others are saying, and prevent us from understanding the validity of others' feelings. As we are taught in James 1:19-20, "Everyone should be quick to listen, slow to speak and slow to become angry, for man's anger does not bring about the righteous life that God desires."

The apostle Paul wrote to the believers at Corinth that he felt afraid when he came to visit them. He feared that he would find them engaging in "quarreling, jealousy, outbursts of anger, factions, slander, gossip, arrogance and disorder" (2 Corinthians 12:20).

Our first responsibility in the group discernment process is to seek the Lord's help in refraining from outbursts of anger.

For some this is very difficult because they feel passionate about certain issues. Others rarely become angry in a discussion, but even those people can lose their composure in certain situations—a process similar to the effect of a catalyst in a chemical reaction.

It is also our responsibility in discernment meetings to pray for those swept up in anger and to find ways to affirm the concern they feel and to translate angry words into more constructive thoughts. This is a great favor to people who let their anger get them off track. It allows the valid thoughts behind the feelings to claim their rightful place in the discourse.

On one occasion, some participants in a church business meeting found themselves unable to channel their emotions constructively. It appeared to one person that the group was headed in an inappropriate direction, and that person gathered up his things and hurried out of the room, slamming the door behind him. The clerk tried to keep the focus on discerning God's leading, but the unconstructive behavior made it difficult. We must not let our passion for a particular outcome get in the way of listening to God and to those speaking God's truth.

3. Is it ever appropriate to vote in a group discernment process? This is not an issue of disobedience to God. After all, Matthias, the apostle selected for the vacancy created by Judas, was picked by the casting of lots. That doesn't seem like a very spiritual process, but God was in it and we assume the apostles made a good choice.

The authors have offered an alternative to voting that avoids the divisions that arise when there is a close vote and keeps the focus on listening to God's voice throughout the process.

4. Can the group discernment process work in large business meetings? In large Christian groups, such as churches with thousands of attendees, most decisions are made in smaller groups; generally the congregation is given a chance to provide input prior to major decisions. But the authors have seen the discernment process work effectively in groups up to five hundred. In a group as large as this, not every one can speak to every issue, but the group can still join in listening to God and can unite around the discerned leading of God.

5. The authors have identified themselves as Quakers, people from a movement that has long experience with discernment. But will these processes work for other Christian groups? We have indicated our background as Quakers and have drawn freely from our experiences in the Friends Church. But we have built our case on Scripture and our experience in group discernment, not on anything unique to being Friends. As we have taught about these processes among folks of other denominations, we have found that they resonate with the ideas and are able to apply them in their own settings.

6. Is it always necessary to express our opposition to a proposal? There are times when one may feel led to say nothing, even when one does not support a proposed action. It may be that the wisdom of the group's action will become more apparent in the future. At other times an individual concludes that his or her misgivings are matters of preference rather than conviction.

Being led not to express one's opposition in the meeting rules out the option of later expressing this opposition and questioning the appropriateness of the group's action. Too many times discussions take place in the parking lot after decisions are made. This kind of second-guessing of decisions harms the group.

7. What if a person feels led to express his or her opposition to an action that is about to be taken? Sometimes an individual senses the need to express a deep hesitation about a planned action. In a voting situation, this wouldn't be necessary because voting "no" provides that opportunity. Quakers have a practice called "standing aside," allowing a person to state his or her concerns and even strong opposition to a course of action that seems to be moving toward approval. The clerk must then determine if more time is needed to discern God's leading. But the clerk must also consider if the person standing aside is doing so because of attentiveness to God's voice or because of stubbornness or personal issues that stand in the way of hearing God's voice.

Before taking the extreme step of standing aside, an individual should examine his or her own discernment process to see if the actions are a response to God's voice or are a result of unhelpful motives. In group discourse not focused on discerning God's leading, it is difficult to back away from strongly expressed positions. Debate is a form of verbal combat and no debater likes to lose. In challenging cases, the opponent of the proposed action continues to say the same things over and over again. In the worst cases, there is a hint or an open threat that the person will leave the group if that person does not get his or her way. This is a sign of dysfunction in the group and should prompt its members to pray for the healing of the individual's spirit and the spirit of the group.

8. Is it ever appropriate to urge a group not to act? Even more unusual than standing aside is the action of an individual who feels very strongly that the group is completely in error in its proposed action. The individual chooses to assume the role of the prophet, asserting that God has spoken to him or her in a way that others have not heard. Such an action must not come from stubbornness or a perverse desire to obstruct. This is not a veto, but a strong caution—a yellow or red light that others will not lightly ignore.

The person with this conviction presents his or her objections, gives the reasons, and asks that the group not move forward with the proposed action. If the group feels led to continue forward despite the objections expressed, the one unable to unite with the action might ask that his or her positions be noted in the meeting's minutes. The dissenting individual may reach the conclusion that he or she cannot for the moment trust the discernment of the group. Therefore, this individual must seek for ways to rebuild that trust and come back into unity with the group in future discernment processes.

SELECTED BIBLIOGRAPHY

The authors have found the following books helpful in their understanding of the processes of individual and group discernment. Many other books on the subject exist for those who wish to deepen their insights.

Anderson, Paul, ed. *Quaker Religious Thought*, no. 106-107 (double issue, November 2006). This special combined issue of the journal contains several articles that are helpful resources: Bruce Bishop, "Discernment—Corporate and Individual Perspectives"; Charles Conniry, "Discernment—Corporate and Individual Considerations"; Paul Anderson, "The Meeting for Worship in which Business Is Conducted"; Eden Grace, "Voting *Not* to Vote: Toward Consensus in the WCC."

Cronk, Sandra L. *Gospel Order: A Quaker Understanding of Faithful Church Community.* Pendle Hill pamphlet 297. Wallingford, Pa.: Pendle Hill Publications, 1991. 48 pages. The authors have found the section on "Gospel Order" as understood by Quakers to be especially helpful.

Dubay, Thomas. *Authenticity: A Biblical Theology of Discernment.* Updated edition. San Francisco: Ignatius Press, 1997 (First edition, 1977). 279 pages. This book contains a more thorough exploration of the theology of discernment than is found in the other books listed here.

Farnham, Suzanne G., Joseph P. Gill, R. Taylor McLean, and Susan M. Ward. *Listening Hearts: Discerning Call in Community.* Revised edition. Harrisburg, Pa.: Morehouse

Publishing, 1991. 145 pages. This book is a result of a thorough collaboration in exploring the concepts of "call," "discernment," and "community," drawing on the Bible and spiritual classics.

Farnham, Suzanne G., Stephanie A. Hull, and R. Taylor McLean. *Grounded in God: Listening Hearts Discernment for Group Deliberations.* Revised edition. Harrisburg, Pa.: Morehouse Publishing, 1999. 106 pages. This is a manual for group discernment, building on the foundation of the ideas in *Listening Hearts.*

Grace, Eden. "Quaker and Ecumenical Essays by Eden Grace," www.edengrace.org. See particularly the essays entitled "Guided by the Mind of Christ—yearning for a new spirituality of church governance," and "An Introduction to Quaker Business Practice."

Green, Tova, and Peter Woodrow. *Insight and Action: How to Discover and Support a Life of Integrity and Commitment to Change.* Philadelphia: New Society Publishers, 1994. 148 pages. This book includes a helpful section on clearness for individual decision making. It also has an appendix with materials from Quakers on clearness and spiritual discernment, including Jan Wood's article, "Spiritual Discernment: The Personal Dimension."

Lonsdale, David. *Listening to the Music of the Spirit: The Art of Discernment.* Notre Dame, Ind.: Ave Maria Press, 1993. 174 pages. The authors are particularly indebted to Lonsdale's summary of Ignatius's teaching on "consolation and desolation" and the place of feelings in discernment.

Loring, Patricia. *Spiritual Discernment: The Context and Goal of Clearness Committees among Friends.* Pendle Hill pamphlet 305. Wallingford, Pa.: Pendle Hill Publications, 1992. 32 pages. This pamphlet, which includes a discussion of the clearness process, is one of several Pendle Hill pamphlets that have helped the authors.

McKinney, Mary Benet. *Sharing Wisdom: A Process for Group Decision Making.* Allen, Tex.: Thomas More Publishing, 1998. 168 pages. McKinney draws on her experience as a

Catholic educator to develop the idea of "shared wisdom" as an alternative to secular, parliamentary decision making.

Morley, Barry. *Beyond Consensus: Salvaging Sense of the Meeting.* Pendle Hill pamphlet 307. Wallingford, Pa.: Pendle Hill Publications, 1993. 32 pages. The authors have been influenced by Morley's discussion on the inadequacies of the idea of consensus and share his preference for the term "sense of the meeting."

Morris, Danny E., and Charles M. Olsen. *Discerning God's Will Together: A Spiritual Practice for the Church.* Nashville: Upper Room Books, 1997. 144 pages. This is one of the most thorough and accessible guides to Christian discernment.

Mueller, Joan. *Faithful Listening: Discernment in Everyday Life.* Kansas City, Mo.: Sheed & Ward, 1996. 136 pages. This is a helpful blend of biblical truth and practical case studies. One of its useful features is its epilogue, entitled "Falling in Love with the Holy Spirit."

Olsen, Charles M. *Transforming Church Boards into Communities of Spiritual Leaders.* Hendron, Va.: The Alban Institute, 1995. 189 pages. Olsen describes an intriguing process of drawing wisdom from biblical stories and from personal experience to lay a foundation for effective discernment in church boards and committees.

Sheeran, Michael J. *Beyond Majority Rule: Voteless Decisions in the Religious Society of Friends.* Denver: Regis College, 1996. 153 pages. Sheeran became dissatisfied with the practice of discernment within his own Catholic tradition and studied the Quaker process of decision making. While it is a very valuable resource, the authors have found it less helpful than some of the other books in our list with regard to the theology of the Holy Spirit guiding believers toward clarity in decision making.

Smith, Gordon T. *Listening to God in Times of Choice: The Art of Discerning God's Will.* Downers Grove, Ill.: InterVarsity Press, 1997. 152 pages. This is a practical and easy-to-read book with a good discussion of various "means" of hearing God and potential blocks to that voice.

Steere, Douglas V. *The Quaker Meeting for Business*. Tallahassee, Fla.: Southeastern Yearly Meeting of the Religious Society of Friends, 1995. Douglas Steere contributed a great deal to Quaker thought and practice, and this short pamphlet, given as a lecture in 1982, includes helpful advice on clerking a Quaker meeting for business.

Wuellner, Flora. "Were Not Our Hearts Burning Within Us?" *Weavings*, vol. 10, no. 5 (Nov./Dec. 1995). Contains a useful section on distinguishing between the voice of the Holy Spirit and other spirits.

CPSIA information can be obtained at www.ICGtesting.com
Printed in the USA
BVOW010149211111

276450BV00001B/13/A